KINGSBARNS

Dr. Ian B. Smith

Published in 2009 by Kingsbarns Community Council History Group
3 Main Street, Kingsbarns, St Andrews, Fife, KY16 9SL with
financial assistance from Awards for All Lottery fund.

British Library Cataloguing-in-Publication Data:
A catalogue record of this booklet is available from the British
Library.
ISBN 978-0-9561304-0-2

Printed in Scotland by Thos McGilvray & Son Ltd, Wemyss Road,
Dysart, Fife, KY1 2XZ.

Cover Illustrations:

Front Cover photography by Sir Peter Erskine, Cambo Estate,
Kingsbarns.
Back Cover photography by Peter Atkin, 3 Main Street, Kingsbarns.

The Kingsbarns History Project

Foreword and Acknowledgments

This project arose out of the wish of a body of the residents of
Kingsbarns and its surrounding area, to record the history of the
village before, as it were, much of the recollections of those still
living there - and elsewhere - are lost to posterity.

The project was initiated through the auspices of the Kingsbarns
Community Council, and the research programme organised by a
History Project Sub-Group. A substantial number of interested
individuals volunteered to research particular aspects of the history
of the village and certain outlying areas and their work is
incorporated in this publication. It has, thus, been the case that my
role has been less than author of this publication than as co-ordinator
of the material produced by these enthusiastic volunteers, and it is
they who deserve the greatest praise. Material which could not be
fitted into the text has been retained, and will be incorporated in a
Kingbarns permanent archive, the location of which has yet to be
decided. Any further information which subsequently comes to light
would be most welcome, and thereafter would then be added to the
archive material.

It was decided by the History Project Sub- Group, and endorsed in
discussion at meetings of the Kingsbarns Community Council, that
the publication should not take the form of a scholarly tome, but
should rather represent a more approachable social history of
Kingsbarns. It was further decided that, while account would be
taken of the origins of the village, and of its place in early Scottish
history, the project would concentrate on the development of the
village and its surroundings in the period broadly since the advent of
the industrial revolution in Britain, ie. from the late 1700s, since

3

which time the social fabric and structure of the UK has changed so substantially.

The study, therefore, emphasises the population changes in the area over the past two hundred years, the alterations in employment patterns over this period, and how the social lives of the villagers have developed in relation to changes in British society as a whole. Much has been made of anecdotes gathered from current village residents, and from others who now live further afield, in order to enliven the text with stories of village life in the recent and more distant past.

There was much discussion on the geographical extent of the study, and it was decided, somewhat reluctantly, that there would have to be a limitation in terms of coverage of the many estates and farms in the Kingsbarns area. It was, therefore decided that, while there may be passing references to estates and farms such as Kippo, Pitmilly and Randerston and Boghall, the Cambo estate would be covered in most detail. The rationalisation for this decision was that much of the ownership of the village and surrounding farmland passed into Cambo ownership over time, including the land on which the Kingsbarns Links golf course was developed, the latter matter in itself forming an integral part of this publication.

It would not have been possible to publish this book without the dedication, enthusiasm and hard work of the research volunteers. Special mention must be made of the technical contribution of the group's Secretary, Peter Atkin, in bringing the project to fruition. The book would not have been possible, moreover, without the contribution from far and wide in the form of pictures, information and memories about Kingsbarns. The staff and pupils of Kingsbarns Primary School, past and present, have also shown an interest which is set to continue. All contributions have been welcomed and appreciated.

Kingsbarns

Contents :

Chapter 1. Scene Setting and Early History 7

Chapter 2. Church and School 20

Chapter 3. Kingsbarns at War 29

Chapter 4. The Cambo Estate 42

Chapter 5. Golf at Kingsbarns 47

Chapter 6. Living in Kingsbarns 58

Final Conclusions 73

Appendix. Chats With Villagers - Past and Present 75

Bibliography 92

Supplementary Illustrations 96

Page

5

Kingsbarns History

Scene Setting and Early History

Introduction

The parish of Kingsbarns lies in the eastern part of the Kingdom of Fife, "...bounded on the north-west by St. Andrews, north-east by the German Ocean, south and south-east by Crail, and west by St. Leonards ...." (Millar, 1895). Following boundary changes in 1891, which saw the inclusion of the farms of East and West Newhall - and the transfer of Grassmiston and Lochton farms to the burgh of Crail - Kingsbarns parish comprised the village itself, and neighbouring farmland, extending to some 4,000 acres. In an area measuring around "...three miles from north-east to south-east, and (some) two and a half miles in breadth..." (Millar, *op. cit*) The population of the parish reached, at its peak in 1831, 1023, was last officially recorded as being 378 in 2006, and is currently estimated at some 380-400 inhabitants.

Early History

Kingsbarns has long had an association with the royalty of Scotland, the castle which was sited between the east part of the village and the sea, being said (Lamont Brown, 2002) to have been a favourite residence of King John Balliol (*r*.1292-96). Indeed, the village is so named because of the area's association with the kings of Scotland, in particular the land's use for the storage, in barns, of grain to service the royal household when in situ at Crail or at Falkland Palace. The castle itself fell into disrepair after the end of the Stuart kings' reign, but, despite its stone being used as building material in the locality (including the harbour), was still partially visible in the mid 19th century.

According to Millar (*Op. Cit*), the earliest known reference to the name of the parish is in a charter of 1519 in which Robert, Duke of Albany, granted sustenance to chaplains to celebrate divine service out of his lands then called *"Kingis-bernis"*. This gift to the Preaching Friars of Fife was maintained by King James III, and was further designated by James V as support for the student members of that order, while studying at the University of St. Andrews. The kings retained substantial lands at what was by then known as Kings Barns and, in the reign of James V, this was tenanted by local families, the principal one of which was the Corstorphines. This family, whose tomb is in Kingsbarns kirkyard (see Illustration A below), held the feu, as was the case with other tenants, on condition that they must serve, when required, in the king's army.

Illustration A

The estate of Kingsbarns formed part of the dowry bestowed by James VI on his Queen, Anne of Denmark. It was then bestowed, by James VI, with his consort's consent, on his chief nurse, Helen Little, thereafter passing to her son, John Gray, reflecting his service to the King. Following the acquisition, in 1669 of the Cambo Estate by Sir Charles Arskine, ownership of the greater part of Kingsbarns passed to what became known as the Erskine family. This state of affairs continued well into the 20th century, until the abolition of the feu system in Scotland in 1975, at which time the land titles were bought by individual families owning properties in the parish.

The Cambo estate itself derives its name from the designation of "de Cambhou" adopted by the descendants of Robert de Newenham, who had received a charter to the lands by King William the Lion. Its ownership thereafter passed through several hands but, since 1688, with a short interlude between 1759 and 1788, has remained with the Erskine family. The original house on the Cambo Estate, built around a 13th century tower, was destroyed by fire in 1878, to be replaced by the extant mansion in 1879-81.

The history of the Cambo lands is covered in more detail later in this volume, but mention should be made here of the other important estates in the locality. The first of these is Pitmilly, situated in the north western portion of the parish, and comprising lands remaining in the hands of one family (the Moneypennys) "…for a longer period, perhaps, than any other estate in Fifeshire." (Millar, *Op. Cit.*). The earliest mention of the estate, cited in Millar, is in 1183, the lands being then given to support the hospital for pilgrims visiting St. Andrews. The canons of St. Andrews held the lands until 1211, when they were acquired by Richard de Monypenny, and the estate remained in this family's hands until the 1940s. We were unable to trace the family line beyond the 1990s. The house, shown in Illustration B, was demolished in 1968 after the failure of a country house hotel venture.

Illustration B

9

The barony of Kippo, sited in the south west part of the parish, can be dated back to the 13th century, the Barclays of Kippo being known to have been in possession in 1285. The estate thereafter passed through several hands, finally being acquired by the Cheape family – the owners also of the Strathtyrum estate near St. Andrews - in 1795, and in whose hands it still lies. Other notable lands in the locality include Randerston, acquired in 1429 by the Myretons (from whom the Erskines bought Cambo) and subsequently by the Balfour family. Randerston House itself has its foundations as a "crowstep gabled 16th century Scots lairds house" (Pevsner, 1988) and now incorporates later additions. Randerston's easterly neighbour, Wormiston, was "owned sporadically by the Balfours and the earls of Lindsay" (Lamont-Brown, 2002), its 17th century house then being acquired, in the 1950s, as residence for the Dowager Lady Erskine. Following her death there in 1953, the house was unused for a further decade before being sold and subsequently restored.

Over the years there have been numerous archaeological discoveries which have provided information as to the earlier inhabitants of the parish area. The most recent of these was the finding, in 2002, of what has become known as the "Kilduncan Stone". This Pictish period stone was found by Mr. Geoff and Mrs Marjorie Lang "...loosely built into a wall in a ruinous outbuilding at their country home of Kilduncan whilst surveying the structure for possible redevelopment..." (Kingdom Magazine, Autumn, 2003). More detail on the stone (shown in Illustration C) may be obtained from the aforementioned article – by Douglas A. Spiers, Fife County Archaeologist. Mr. Spiers estimates that the stone may be dated to the 9th or early 10th century, and is an extremely rare example of early Christian sculpture. Given its importance, it was declared as "treasure trove" and is now on loan at St. Andrews Museum in Kinburn House.

ILLUS 16 Drawing of Kilduncan 1C

Illustration C

Other recent discoveries have included a 4,000 year old pot uncovered by workmen at Pitmilly, also in 2002, and a number of significant items which came to light during the construction of the new golf links. Comprehensively covered in a paper by Heather F. James, which appeared in the Tayside and Fife Archaelogical Journal (Vol. 7, 2001), the principal finds on the golf course site were "…an Iron Age short cist burial, prehistoric pits, and a buried eighteenth century bridge."

Illustration D shows the locations of the finds, and also gives an indication of the site of the long defunct Kingsbarns Castle. The short cist burial was, in fact, found by a member of the public, David

11

Finlay, while walking his dog. Subsequent pathological analysis concluded that the skeleton in the burial cist was that of a young woman and, despite the absence of supporting artefacts, can be dated back to the early Iron Age. As before, much more detail on the archaeological excavations which followed the discoveries may be found in Dr. James' paper and readers seeking a more academic account should access this source. Here, a final point worthy of mention is that the discovery of the long covered over 18th century bridge was a delight to the golf club developers, who have now made it an attractive feature on the course (between the 18th green and the clubhouse).

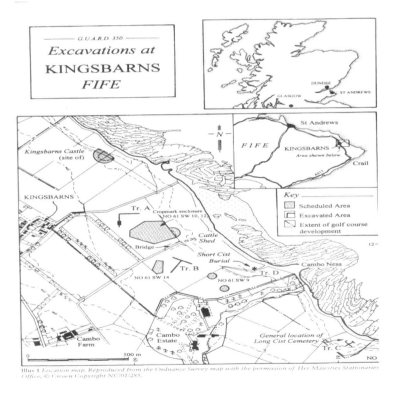

Illustration D

Kingsbarns Village

With regard to the village itself, the layout has changed over time, as comparison even between the 1895 map, at Illustration E, and a recent aerial photograph, at Illustration F, will show. The principal differences have been the construction of new dwellings, including relatively small scale Council housing, and the (sympathetic) conversion of former farm buildings into domestic houses. It should be noted that, since the village gained conservation status, in 1970, new developments have been subject to greater scrutiny than had previously been the case, hence minimising the degree of visual impact of the recent 'new builds'.

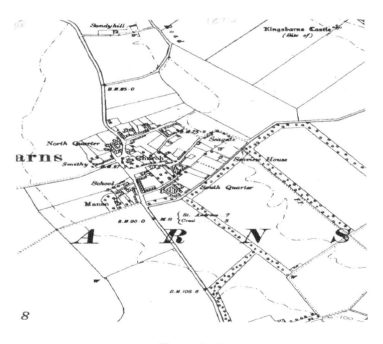

Illustration E

Irrespective of the recent developments, the Square remains the village's central feature, and on it sit Kingsbarns Parish Church and Kingsbarns House. The Church will be further covered in this volume, but the salient facts are that its origins date back to 1631, the year in which Kingsbarns was disjoined from Crail Parish. Pevsner

(1988) notes its design to be a "(harled) T-plan" since when the original church spire has been heightened three times, being finally extended to its current elevation in 1866. The principal alterations to the church were those of 1810-11, undertaken by John Corstorphine, arcthitect/builder, and Robert Balfour, the latter also being responsible for the remodelling of the aforementioned Pitmilly House.

In the centre of the Square stands the village pump, dated 1831, and to its east is Kingsbarns House. The principal house dates originally from the mid 18th century, but it was reconstructed by and for the occupancy of John Corstorphine around 1794 (this date being carved on the frieze of the corniced doorpiece (Pevsner, 1988). Corstorphine was also responsible for the design of Kingsbarns School (on Main Street). School life is dealt with later in this account, suffice, at this point, to state that it is the oldest school in Fife still in service, the use of the current building dating originally to 1822.

Illustration F

14

Other notable buildings in the square include Wellgate, described by Pevsner as having a "18th century harled crowstepped gable...on to the square". In fact, the section of the house facing the square is 18th century, but the part looking on to Main Street was actually built in the 19th century, in 18th century style. It is interesting to note that Wellgate, up to the 1950s, had a grocer's shop integrated into the section of the house facing the square. Abutting Wellgate on the east side of the square is Cessneuk, a further 18th century mansion, completing a pleasing façade as one enters the square from the Crail Road. Finally, in the Square, there should be mention of No 1, the old schoolhouse, to which further mention will be made in the section on 'Church and School'.

Opposite the Church is another group of interesting houses, worthy of mention. The first of these is North Quarter, described by Pevsner as "a smart early 19th century farmhouse, with a pantiled steading behind." This latter steading has, in fact, been redeveloped recently as housing, in a style sympathetic to the local architecture. To the north of North Quarter, down what is known locally as Torrie Wynd, stands Torrie House, another handsome early 19th century house (Pevsner). Also in this part of the village, opposite North Quarter, and to the north of the church is the 'Cambo Arms' (recently renamed) - a late 18th or early 19th century coaching inn which Pevsner describes as "contemporary with, but plainer than, North Quarter".

Further interesting houses in this part of the village are on Station Road, including The Pleasaunce, now one house, but at one time divided into two dwellings. One of these incorporated a 'sweetie shop', much frequented by the local children. Finally, at 3 Station Road, stands 'The Smithy', another smart house with a cow byre and blacksmith's shop adjoining.

The "new" Manse, off Main Street in the direction of Crail, was erected in 1837 in plain, late Georgian style. This new Manse, originally built as a single property, has since been divided into 2 dwellings. Other interesting late 18th and early 19th century buildings are in and around the Seagate, including "The Grey House", dating from 1793. On Seagate there is also a 17th century house which was restored, in 1976, by The National Trust for Scotland. At the time of its reconstruction this house was divided into two dwellings, one being named 'Monypenny House' (see the "before and after" pictures at Illustration G below), although there is no record of any earlier connection with the aforementioned Monypennys of Pitmilly, and the other 'Mill House' in recognition of the working (travelling) mill which had previously existed on the site.

Illustration G

Other buildings worthy of note include the originally named Briar Rose and Croft Cottage, on Smiddy Burn - this street having recently re-acquired its former name after being known for many years as North Street. This particular house was built in 1792 for a Pittenweem sea captain and his wife, Croft Cottage being added for their adult daughter. Elsewhere, on Smiddy Burn are two 18th century adjoining houses, one unnamed, but the other known as May Cottage. Smiddy Burn has further buildings of note, including 'The Old Forge', dating from 1792 - the earliest of the three blacksmiths in the village - and portrayed by Pevsner as " pantiled (but originally thatched) with scrolled skewputts". Sweet Hope Cottage is also worth mentioning, given that it is of similar date to The Old Forge opposite. Of more recent vintage, California House, also on Smiddy Burn, is built around the foundations of a much earlier house, while the street, finally, boasts a splendid late 1920s house, Croft Butts, built in the English country style of the time.

On another village street, Back Stile, are two further interesting houses. The first is South Quarter, attached to what was, at one time, the third farm in Kingsbarns, Pevsner deeming it "a very plain farmhouse dated 1786". The other is an imposing Victorian villa, now called Greenloaning. Rumour had it that this latter house was built by the clerk of works rebuilding Cambo House (after its disastrous fire) for his own use. The author has established that it was, in fact, built by a grandfather of Bill Swan (see 'Chats with Villagers' later in this volume) while he was working with the architect, Robert Lorimer, later knighted, on the 1884 extensions to Cambo House.

Returning to Main Street, a further two buildings are of interest. The first is the house and outbuildings called Crombie's Hall, which sits directly opposite the village shop and Post Office. The title deeds for this house date back to 1714, although the current buildings are predominantly of 19th century design. It is thought that the name derives from the wife of the first owner, who was called Hellen Crumie. Lived in continuously since 1938 by the Bell family, it was both a dwelling house and the business premises of John Bell, the foremost joiner in the village. Also on Main Street stands the Kingsbarns Memorial Hall, originally opened in 1954 (this opening shown in Illustration H) - and containing the Memorial plaque to those who fell in service in the Second World War - it was refurbished in the late 1990s and reopened in 2000 by the MP for North East Fife, (now Sir) Menzies Campbell. The Hall serves a vital purpose in village life, as the venue for many charity events, WRI meetings, the annual Flower Show, Community Council and other such assemblies.

Illustration H

Finally, on Main Street, is the village shop and Post Office which, incorporating the adjoining house (dating from 1826) occupies Nos 11-15. Formerly, however, the Post Office was at No 9 Main Street and, although the date of the original establishment of postal services in the village is not known, there is evidence from the 1881 Census that there was a postmistress residing at, and operating from 9, Main Street at that time.

Summary

This initial section has sought to put Kingsbarns Parish in context, encompassing a brief history of the principal estates, and the establishment of the village itself. This volume is not intended, however, as an account merely of the architecture and buildings of the locality. It is, rather, aimed at recounting the lives and experiences of those who have inhabited the area, most particularly in the period since the beginning of the 19th century. It is, thus, to these matters that we now turn.

Church and School

There is evidence that the activities of church and school have been inextricably linked over the centuries. Thus, in this volume, they are being considered together in the same section of the text. To begin with the parish church (seen at Illustration I), its history dates to its disjoining, in 1631, from Crail church under whose jurisdiction it had existed since medieval times. Pevsner describes the church building as a "harled T-plan kirk, …much altered in 1810", and whose spire was raised in height, significantly, (Pevsner, rather uncharitably, deeming it an "ungainly top"), in 1866. Its churchyard contains graves dating from 1633, an inventory of which was compiled by John Bell, father of the current village residents, Margaret and Jean (cited at various points in this volume), and which will also form part of the Kingsbarns archive. Its south wall also has mounted on it the memorial, referred to in the section on "Kingsbarns at War", to those village residents who lost their lives serving in the First World War.

Illustration I

For a church with such a long history, it has had remarkably few ministers, the period from 1632 to 1974 seeing only eleven incumbents to that position. The publication "Crail Church through the centuries" (1999), has these Kingsbarns ministers listed, and they include the Reverends George Wright and Alexander Todd whose consecutive service lasted from 1809 to 1926. The Revd. Dr. Wright served for sixty years (1809-1869), and his successor, the Revd. Dr. Todd for fifty seven years (1869-1926). They were then followed by Douglas Bisset who was parish minister from 1926 until 1974. That year marked the return of Kingsbarns church to the Crail church fold, as it were, with the re-linking of the two churches. There have since been two more holders of the post of parish minister. The current incumbent, Mike Erskine, was installed as Minister in 2002.

While not the original manse, the most significant, and long used building was that of 1834-5, set back slightly from Main Street in the direction of Crail (previously described in the introduction to this volume). It accommodated the long serving ministers through the remainder of the 19th century, and up to the rejoining of the church with Crail. Although a grand house by any standards, and certainly much better appointed than its predecessor, the long serving Revd. Dr. Wright (see Illustration J) apparently considering that it was more suitable than the former manse, but then they did have 14 children…

Illustration J

21

The Ladies' Work Party

The Work Party was established in 1907 by the ladies of the village, in conjunction with the church, in order to support deserving causes. Each lady made a personal contribution to the funding of the enterprise, thought to be either 1/- or 2/6d, and the Kirk Session put up a further £1.

The total raised came to the sum of £3-4/6d, and a portion was soon used to buy materials, specifically linen and flannel, for the ladies to make goods for a sale. This first sale was duly held in June 1908, the ladies buying 10lbs. of cake and eighty buns (costing some 8/4d) for the teas. The sale was held in the school hall and, despite other costs - cleaning, the hire of china and cutlery - raised the not inconsiderable sum of £25-10s.

The causes supported by the Work Party were both local and national/international. Local interests favoured by its Committee were such as the alleviation of poverty in the parish, the Aged and Infirm Ministers Fund, and the Temperance Association. On a wider front, the kirk connections led to support being given to foreign missions of the Church of Scotland, while the First World War period saw contributions being made to various parts of the war effort, such as the War Fund, the Nursing Fund, and the Disabled Soldiers and Sailors Fund.

1927 brought a new minister, and new ideas as to the purpose of the Work Party. Under the auspicies of the Reverend Bisset, the funds became more clearly directed towards church related causes, such as the Fabric Fund, and towards china expenses. Further funds were used for, for example a Pulpit Bible, a brass reading desk, and rush matting for the choir and stair area of the church, as well as were specified for the purchase of two brass vases – still used in the kirk today – for the sum of £3-2/6d. Illustration K, shows the Womens' Rural Institute (WRI), taken in the 1920s/30s, with Lady Erskine seated far right (photograph taken in the village school).

Illustration K

The pattern of Work Party donations began to change again into the 1930s, with non-directly local causes being supported, such as Jewish Missions, the Nursing Association, and World Missions, as well as quasi-local sources as Dundee Royal Infirmary. This latter spread of interests covered continued until the 1950s, by which time the National Health Service had been established.

The 1960s saw continuation of the local/international contribution split, with the sales - now raising some some £300-400 each - utilised both for local causes such as the Church Clock Fund, donations for the Sunday School and Bible Class, as well as the hitherto wider community of Church of Scotland communities worldwide.
After the retiral of the Reverent Bisset in 1974, the Work Party group had to find a new venue for their meetings, settling on the home, Jorach, of a then active member, Mrs. Rachel Brown. Sales were, by then, realising around £1,000 each, and such fund-raising activities were supplemented by other events such as Strawberry Teas, Fashion Shows, Flower Festivals, and Bridge Parties.

Donations in the recent past have continued to be a mix of local and more diverse causes. Thus, the village kirk has continued to benefit from contributions towards furniture and carpet replacements, as have other newer churches in the New Towns of Fife. Other local charities have also benefited, such as Maggie's Centre in Kirkcaldy, while more international causes such as the Asian 'tsunami', African Famine Relief, and other disaster relief initiatives have also been supported.

Overall, the Work Party has had a very significant impact on village affairs, and has also supported a wide range of international causes, while providing a focus for companionship amongst its members, and a sense of achievement from the giving of time and talent to help create a better world.

As for the village school, by comparison with the church, the current edifice is a mere stripling, being "only" 187 years old. However, having been established in 1822, as previously stated, it is the oldest school in Fife still in operation. Pevsner is quite complimentary on the school, describing it as "Small and pretty, with an ogee-roofed bellcote…". There is, however, evidence of school buildings being present much earlier in the village, dating back to much closer to the establishment of the church. From the Kirk Session Minutes, indeed, it is evident that a school existed from around 1667, with parents being encouraged to insist that their children attend.

A more recent memento of the school history is referred to in Illustration L, showing Bill Swan, son of the builder who maintained the school over a large number of years - and who had built the cupola for the school bell - in discussion with various children. The context for their chat was a proposal to reinstate the bell in time for the new millennium, but, on inspection, it was found that the bell-tower was in a dangerous state of disrepair, and it had to be dismantled and rebuilt before a new bell and cupola were finally installed in 2001. Bill was further involved in that he unveiled the new cupola, replacing the previous one made by his father.

Pupils saved by the bell!

GETTING a history lesson on the bell tower at Kingsbarns School, from villager Bill Swan whose father built the tower, are (clockwise from left) Karmen Donald P2, Kirsty Mitchell P1, Paul Rennie P6, Emily Wheelan P4 and Steven Calander P4.

However, plans to replace the bell in time for the millennium revealed that the structure of the tower was unsafe and could have collapsed, with possible tragic consequences in the playground.

See story on page 3

Illustration L

The current school roll, reflecting the fall in the village population, is 'only' 30, although this is higher than the figure of 7 in 1996. The school was originally built to accommodate some 200 children and, although this number of pupils was never quite reached, the school populace reached its peak in the late 1800s - the actual peak being 143 children in 1889. Pressure on facilities is noted in the School Board records of 1878, when it was noted that the growing number of pupils had meant that an extension of ground had been required "for a playground for the scholars, and for a residence for the teacher(s) in the school". This was provided, at that time, by land sold by the Erskines of Cambo to the School Board. Illustration M shows the (large number of) school pupils lining up on a section of Main Street in the early 1900s (the photograph is wrongly described as being taken on Station Road – although that can be seen in the background) for an unknown occasion.

Illustration M

The last but one schoolhouse to be occupied by a resident teacher was the house situated at No1, The Square. It is still in existence, and its outward appearance little altered from when it was built. It is also positive to note that its current owners, Mr. and Mrs. Duncan, are endeavouring to return many of the external and internal features of the house. Although it is not thought that he was housed in this particular schoolhouse, one of the most eminent schoolmasters was Alexander Latto, who – will be covered in the section on "Golf at Kingsbarns"- was also the first long serving Secretary of the Kingsbarns Golfing Society, and whose elaborate headstone in the churchyard is further commented on in the golfing material.

Mr. Latto also had a son, Thomas Carstairs Latto, who became a renowned poet and songwriter, and who emigrated to the USA. Many of his poems and songs appeared in a wide variety of publications, including Tait's Magazine in Scotland, and Harper's Magazine in the USA. Some of his later songs were also included in the Book of Scottish Song.

Moving to more recent times, there are interesting accounts of school life which are worthy of mention. Malcolm Campbell, for example, was a pupil in the WW2 years, and can recall a "busy, well populated school, with children attending from the village itself and from the outlying farms such as Cambo, Randerston, Kippo, Boghall and Hillhead". The school roll was also increased by the presence of the evacuees who, as is later mentioned, came, mainly, from Edinburgh.

The schoolmaster of that time was Mr. William Wilkie who, as recounted by Malcolm Campbell, was very active in the life of the village "…being Elder and Session Clerk of the church, Secretary/Treasurer of the Men's Club, Secretary/Treasurer of the Village Hall, and Secretary/Treasurer of Kingsbarns Golf Club", amongst other such similar positions. One of Mr. Wilkie's wartime roles, moreover, was the teaching of English to the Polish soldiers stationed nearby, their lessons taking place after the finish of the regular lessons.

Betty Kitchin started school slightly later than Malcolm Campbell, in 1952, and recalls there being two parts to the school buildings. At that time the "main school building on the left contained two classrooms and the dining room, and the harled building to the right which was a dual purpose classroom/gym hall at the front with the staffroom, play sheds, toilets, and boiler house to the rear." There were two teachers then - the Head Teacher, who lived in the schoolhouse previously described in The Square, and the Infant teacher, who travelled in from St. Andrews. Interestingly, there were relatively few children resident in the village, so that the majority of the pupils came from the neighbouring farms.

There were several consequences from this fact. One was that, as a result of the trend towards farm workers moving often from one employer to another, there was a high rate of pupil turnover at the school. The teachers also had to cope with the related changing mix of ages of children at the school, making teaching more difficult, and without much consistency over time. A more mundane, but still were often sent home after "dinner" and/or didn't come to school at all.

While these seem negative points, Betty Kitchin also points out that there were also enjoyable elements to education at Kingsbarns primary. These positive experiences of more recent pupils of the school, are noted below; first of these being George Sutherland, who was a pupil between 1955 and 1962. George, whose father was employed by Sir David Erskine at Cambo, and whose family stayed at Cambo Gardens, recalls enjoying doing P.E. in the school gymhall, and also watching films which were brought into the school once a month. Such comments are echoed by other pupils from the same era, such as George's sister, Beryl, and by Jean Bell, all of whom remember particular teachers eg. Mr Wilkie, the Headmaster, Miss McCawley, and Mrs. Cunningham - Beryl Sutherland remembering in particular the latter teacher's lessons about wildlife. More recent comments from former pupils would include those of Emily Cobb, one of the village's eminent families, whose memories from her time at the village school include the positive elements of small classes, very good supply teachers, and a sympathetic working environment.

Summary :

There has been a close working relationship between the church and school since the establishment of the former in 1631. It has been seen that there is evidence of the setting up of a local school not many years after the church was established, and, although the existing school can be dated 'only' back to 1822, it appears that a form of school existed in the village back to, at least, the 1660s. The church/school/ Community Council triumvirate is also still in vigorous existence, looking after local interests in these respects.

KINGSBARNS AT WAR

Introduction :

The rural status of the village and the outlying farms and estates meant that a substantial proportion of the inhabitants were granted exempt status from front line duties during both the First and Second World Wars. However, a significant number of the young men volunteered to serve in WW1, including Major Sir T. Erskine of Cambo, and Captain G. J. Todd, the son of the Kirk Minister. Those individuals, together with the other volunteers are listed as such in the Roll of Honour 1914-1918 in Kingsbarns Parish Church. Fifteen of their number fell in action, their names being further honoured in the War Memorial on the exterior of the Church, shown at Illustration N.

Illustration N

One of the fallen, Bombardier Thomas Pearson McDonald of the Royal Field Artillery, one of many to have died at the Battle of the Somme, is shown, as a young boy, in the attached family photograph. His death notice is also shown in Illustration O.

Casualty Details

Name: McDONALD, THOS PEARSON
Initials: T P
Nationality: United Kingdom
Rank: Bombardier
Regiment/Service: Royal Field Artillery
Unit Text: "B" Bty. 256th Bde.
Age: 22
Date of Death: 21/08/1917
Service No: 636635
Additional information: Son of Thos. McDonald. Native of Kingsbarns, Fifeshire.
Casualty Type: Commonwealth War Dead
Grave/Memorial Reference: V. E. 9.
Cemetery: VLAMERTINGHE NEW MILITARY CEMETERY

Illustration O

During the First World war – and, as we will see later in WW2 – the village and surrounding farms were also heavily involved in the war effort in supplying food produce to the urban centres servicing the

30

front line operations. The local populace were also involved in WW1 in other, less likely ways, as the following stories illustrate.

The Wrecking of HMS Success

HMS Success (pictured in Illustration P) was a small destroyer, built in Sunderland in 1901/2. Although considered technically "obsolete" by then, she had already seen action in the early stages of the First World War prior to the Kingsbarns incident. In the early hours of 3rd. November 1914 the destroyer had been involved in the successful repelling of an attack by the German fleet on Great Yarmouth (1). HMS Success had been part of a flotilla of four destroyers which encountered eight German naval vessels intent on attacking Yarmouth. Although in the successful defence, she may not have been in range to fire her own guns, Success is likely to have been the target of gunfire from the German fleet (2), albeit that she suffered no damage.

Illustration P

Alas, after this gallant action, HMS Success had but only some six weeks remaining in her contribution to the war effort when, having lost her course in the wartime blackout, she was wrecked off Kingsbarns (3) in early morning, 27th December 1914. The ship's Lieutenant in Command's Report (4) indicates that the vessel ran aground at around 4.50am. on 27th. December 1914, on a voyage originating in Aberdeen and with a proposed destination of Rosyth. On the event of the grounding, a nearby destroyer, HMS Mallard, was alerted by an SOS sent by Success' Lieutenant in Command and, it relatively soon becoming clear that it would be necessary to abandon ship, rocket signals were fired to activate responses from neighbouring lifeboat stations.

Given that the First World War was firmly in progress, and that the East Coast of Scotland offered vulnerable targets, it is hardly surprising that the signals caused great consternation amongst the inhabitants of the immediate locality. It soon transpired however, that this was not a German attack, but a British naval vessel in distress. Lifeboats were, therefore, dispatched from both St. Andrews and Crail, the latter arriving on the scene at about 9am. (5).

There being sixty seven officers and crew on board Success, and the capacity of the Crail lifeboat being a maximum of twenty, there had to be three rescue trips, taking all but the Lieutenant in Command and twelve seamen the 500 yards to safety on Kingsbarns foreshore. During these dangerous missions, the Crail lifeboat's coxswain, Andrew Cunningham, was swept overboard, as was crew member, Charles Dewar. Both, however, were rescued, and they and all 54 seamen thus survived the incident, albeit some with minor injuries. There remained on board, however, thirteen sailors, Lieutenant Pennefather included. It was, therefore, timely for those left on board, that the St. Andrews lifeboat then arrived at the wreck, particularly as the Crail lifeboat had been incapacitated by having been "…dashed against the rocky beach." (6). Although it was reported that the commander "prevaricated" for some time as to what course of action he wished to sanction (7), those thirteen finally boarded the St. Andrews lifeboat which was towed back to St. Andrews by the destroyer HMS Cheerful.

A number of those taken to St. Andrews remained there, to be billeted for the night. However, Lieutenant Pennefather formed a "working party", himself and several of his crew thus returning to Kingsbarns, arriving at 2.30pm.(8).This group immediately began salvage work on the vessel, including assessing the prospect of being able to re-float her.

In the meantime, the fifty four seamen saved earlier made their way into Kingsbarns village, but not before giving "...three rousing cheers for the lifeboat-men." (9)The Citizen (op. cit.) also notes that their journey to the village from the foreshore was aided by a number of "conveyances", arranged by Lloyds' agent in Crail (10), and on their arrival in the village they were greeted by the entire Kingsbarns' populace. The village school was co-opted as a shelter for the seamen, who were given food and warm drinks and, where necessary, clothing to replace that which had been lost in the wreck. Once revived, the able-bodied officers and crew then returned to the shore to assist with the securing of the vessel, and in beginning the task of landing torpedoes, guns, and other valuable equipment. However, while Lieutenant Pennefather and some crew members remained until 31st. December to continue the salvage work, the bulk of the seamen were transported to St. Andrews on the Sunday night (27th. December) by the motor transports of the Highland Cyclist Battalion which was stationed in the area. Before their departure, the then Parish Church Minister, the Reverend Alexander Todd, delivered an address, in the school, to the officers and men in which the village resounded to the strains of the hymn, Abide with Me.(11) On the issue of the departure of the Success officers and crew, the Citizen (op.cit.) further reported that "...as each vehicle left, the navymen stood up and cheered the throng of villagers, who pressed gifts and warm wraps upon the sailors." The Lieutenant in Command, meantime, states in his Report (12) that he returned to Rosyth on Ist. January 1915 without any reference as to whether or not there had been any further contact between himself and the villagers prior to his departure.

Although Lieutenant Pennefather's return to base at Rosyth was some days after the rest of his officers and crew, the fact that he did not remain further, while initiated by Admiralty orders, was influenced by the final judgment that it was becoming increasingly unlikely that the destroyer was going to be refloated. (13). This negative interpretation proved to be correct, and what was left after the salvage operation remains to this day stranded in the sands off Kingsbarns beach.

The remains of the vessel can still be seen, its location being close to the bathing danger marker pole in a southerly direction. It is only, however, visible at extremely low water, and only then when movements in the sand clarify its position. Illustration Q provides a representation of the wreck at its clearest , the most prominent features when most exposed being the steel casting supporting the screws and rudder(s), resembling a double swan neck protruding from the water – as seen in the photograph. On occasions, the engine mountings and propeller-shaft area, and the keel, which points out to sea, may also be observed.

Illustration Q

The aspects of the hulk visible from the shore notwithstanding, there is little memorabilia from the wreck known to exist. However, the next 3 illustrations show artefacts which a local collector (and contributor to this volume) Andy Sherriff has established came from materials on HMS Success. Thus, Illustration R shows a table made from timber taken from the vessel, Illustration S being a lock (perhaps from a cabin door), while T is a seaman's whistle which Andy's family records indicate was given to his grandfather by one of the Success' crew at the time of the rescue.

Illustration R

Illustration S

Illustration T

As for the cause of the wreck, the subsequent Court of Enquiry (held with alacrity on 2nd. January 1915) decided that Lieutenant Pennefather was to be informed that be was being blamed for a series of navigational errors (14) which had led to the loss of the vessel. However, it was decided not to proceed with a Court Martial, partly for logistical reasons, but also to take into account the judgment that, as commanding officer, Lieutenant Pennefather "…showed much energy and resolve after the wreck."(15).

Admiral Lowry's Report for the Admiralty also commends the actions of the Crail and St. Andrews lifeboats which "…did excellent service, incurring great danger.." (16). While not specifically mentioned in the Admiralty material already cited, there is little doubt that the Navy also, implicitly, also owed a debt of gratitude to the people of Kingsbarns.

Under the sub-heading of "Kindly Treated at Kingsbarns", The Citizen article previously referred to of 2nd. January 1915 (*op. cit.*) refers to the aforementioned provision of food, shelter, clothing and transport by Kingsbarns residents which must have greatly alleviated the suffering of the seamen involved in the wreck.

The "Aviation Rescue"

A further example of positive involvement in the First World War effort by Kingsbarns residents was not long coming. Within days of the heroics involved in the HMS Success rescue - indeed on the day on which Lieutenant Pennefather departed for Rosyth, 1st. January 1915 - the Kingsbarns based yawl, the "Barbara ", was instrumental in effecting the rescue of two airmen whose plane had plunged into the sea, some one and a half miles off Kingsbarns.

The aviators had set off from Dundee in search of any German craft in the area but the gale force conditions resulted in their potentially disastrous situation in the waters in Kingsbarns bay. Despite these severely adverse weather conditions, and in a comparatively small vessel (a 17 feet keel), Messrs. Robert Brown and Archibald Ritchie put to sea and succeeded in getting the two aviators on board. They then found that they could not return to Kingsbarns, and it required the St. Andrews lifeboat – skippered by one of the previous week's heroes, Coxwain Chisholm – to accompany the Barbara to St. Andrews. Mr. Brown was later awarded a silver medal in recognition of his bravery, The Citizen of 6th. March 1915 reporting Sheriff Armour-Hanney as saying that he and the assembled company "..wished (Mr. Brown) would be long spared to wear it, and that he would hand it down as an inspiration to those who were to come after him." (17).

The Second World War

As regards the Second World War, it is recorded that a considerable number of the local men and young women were called up for active service. In addition some others were recruited to serve in such capacities as personnel serving the local airfields. Of those who served in the Armed Forces, ten lost their life – including two from the same (Brown) family, and their valiant efforts are recorded in the War Memorial (pictured in Illustration U) in the Kingsbarns Memorial Hall.

Illustration U

Village life during the Second World War was affected in many ways, both in the sense of the gearing of agricultural production directly to the war effort, and in the operation of ancillary facilities on behalf of the Armed Forces. Examples of the latter were the wireless station, now cottages just outside the village towards the Cambo estate, and the associated airfield at North Quarter farm. The wireless station was linked to HMS Jackdaw at Crail Airfield , whose activities are well documented in Malcolm Fife's book on "Crail and Dunino" airfields.(17).

Local residents recall the impact which the airfield sites - and the wider war situation - had on village life. Malcolm Campbell, and Robert Bell, for example, both remember the arrival, and stay of Polish Army soldiers, who were billeted at and around Dunino Airfield. Fife (2003) shows clearly the harsh living conditions which were endured by the Polish forces, but there are fond memories of their social interaction with local residents. Both villagers cited above have very positive recollections of the generosity of the Polish airmen, who "hosted" a party for local children at Pitmilly House (with presents for children who had to do with little luxury during the war years), and, in particular, the Bell family were recipients of a horse and carriage made by them for their then young son, Robert.

The Bell family also recall the billeting of Italian prisoners of war in their house, who worked as labourers for their joiner father and had to be locked in at night, but who found the time to cook spaghetti and interact socially with parents and children. There were also evacuees to the village, mainly from Edinburgh, who were looked after by local families. One such example, as recalled by Malcolm Campbell, were a brother and sister, Alan and Muriel Berry, who stayed with the Campbell family, and who, eventually, emigrated to Canada.

Other residents of the time recall how the village was affected by the war. Social life, as with most such other rural communities, went on as best it could. The WRI and the local Men's Club continued their activities throughout the war. The WRI, for example, was held on the Wednesdays of the full moon so that rural women could walk safely home. Dances were also held regularly for locals and service personnel in various locations, including the old Hall, the school, and Pitmilly House.

The Second World War brought with it this social camaraderie which helped local cohesion, other examples being dances held at the Old Hall (now North Quarter) attended by sailors and men from the Dunino Airfield and from the wireless station. However, the war also brought privations, for example the construction of coastal defences prepared in the possible event of a German invasion. These defensive procedures also resulted in the loss of the original Kingsbarns golf links, which were mined. Residents missed their contact with the local beach, which was "out of bounds" due to the war restrictions and it was only in the latter years of the war that a judgment of a German invasion becoming a much less likely event meant that the local populace regained their access to the beach area. The (re)construction of the golf course took rather longer. As will be covered later, it was not until the year 2000 that Kingsbarns Golf Links was completed.

Summary

Although, essentially a rural community, Kingsbarns was by no means untouched by the events of the two World Wars. As happened in countless other communities, WW1 saw the selfless volunteering of large numbers of young men and women and, as has already been recounted, a substantial proportion of those who offered to serve lost their life in the conflict. The Second World War differed in that there was conscription in place throughout the conflict and, although many young people were exempted from active service, village and farm life was still affected by the displacement of those chosen to serve – and by the operation of ancilliary services both in Kingsbarns itself, and in the surrounding area.

Endnotes to the HMS Success story:

(1) The German raid was undertaken in the mistaken belief that there was a significant defence works at Yarmouth.

(2) The end result of the skirmish was that the German ships turned for home, believing that the British fleet was considerably stronger than the four destroyers which comprised the local defence.

(3) The exact location of the grounding, according to Statement of Information submitted by Lieutenant in Command, Wm. Pennefather, was Kings Barnes (*sic*) boat harbour, N30 W, 300 yards. Taken from Enclosure 2, Admiralty Commanding, Coast of Scotland, 7th. January 1915.

(4) Report to Vice Admiral, commanding 3rd. Battle Squadron, HMS King Edward VII, 1st. January 1915, p.2.

(5) Nearer 8am. according to The Citizen, 2nd. January 1915. The Crail lifeboat's arrival would have been sooner had it not been for wartime   restrictions on the use of flares, requiring the coxswain to call at the houses of all 12 crew members individually, thereby delaying their departure. (op. cit.)

(6) Op. cit.

(7) An account in The East of Fife Record, December 31st. 1914, reports that it was some forty five minutes before Leiutenant Pennefather agreed to board the St. Andrews lifeboat, thus placing in jeopardy the safety not only of himself and his crew, but also the brave souls manning the St. Andrews lifeboat.

(8) Pennefather Report (*op.cit.*).

(9) The Citizen (*op.cit.*). A commendably speedy response to the crisis, although rather glossed over in The Citizen article (*op. cit.*).

(10)*Op. Cit.*

(11)Lieutenant Pennefather Report, *op.cit.* p.4.

(12)Pennefather Report, *op.cit.*, entry for 31st. December, "Went down to ship at 6.0am. and found the Engine Room flooded which left little able to be done." *op.cit.*,p4.

(13)Findings of the Court of Enquiry, held on HMS Zealandia, 2nd. January 1915, p.2

(14)Admiralty Report, Admiral R.S. Lowry, 7th. January 1915.

(15)*op.cit.* Coxwain Cunningham was, in fact, further rewarded for his gallant efforts to save the crew of HMS Success by the subsequent award of an RNLI silver medal, and his own crew sent a cheque for £7 from the officer's mess of the cape Light Horse Regiment of South Africa

(16)The Citizen, 6th. March 1915. As in the case of Coxwain Cunningham, it was the RNLI silver medal which was awarded to Robert Brown.

(17)Malcolm Fife, Crail and Dunino. The Story of Two Scottish airfields Airfields, 2003, GMS Enterprises, Peterborough.

Note: Published too late for incorporation into this account of the wreck of HMS Success is the book by Bob Baird, "Shipwrecks of the Forth and Tay". It is, however, included in the Bibliography of this volume, and those interested in the topic should access Mr Baird's book.

The Cambo Estate

As was mentioned in the introductory chapter to this volume, the Cambo Estate came into the possession of the Erskine family in 1669, the first owner being Sir Charles Arskine who, at that time, held the post of Lord Lyon King at Arms. The estate was sold, in 1759, to the Cherteris family (who came from East Lothian) but was then bought back in 1788 by the ninth Earl of Kellie, Thomas Erskine - cousin of the former owners - and the family has maintained ownership, and occupancy ever since.

The ninth Earl of Kellie, who had regained the estate for the family was married, but had no children through his wife. He had a daughter, Anna Eglehart, prior to his marriage however, and he and his wife then adopted all of his daughter's children, through which the family line has since descended. The oldest "son" became the first baronet of Cambo in 1821 and he - and his successor - provide the first link with golf in the region, both being Captains of the Royal and Ancient (R & A) Golf club of St. Andrews. Portraits of both hang in the new clubhouse of the Kingsbarns Golf Links. As will be further discussed in the section on "Golf at Kingsbarns", the family authorised the establishment of the original Kingsbarns golf course, and the estate still owns the land on which the new Kingsbarns Golf Links was constructed.

There are plentiful war connections with the estate and the family. During the Napoleonic Wars, for example, much timber was taken for ship construction. In the First World War, Sir Thomas Erskine served as Colonel in the Scottish Horse Regiment and he and his batman, Bill Greig - forebear of a local family - took part in the Gallipoli campaign. Incidentally, Sir Thomas is credited as being the first domestic car owner in Fife, and acted as the county's road convenor - and the family still owns the number plate of that first car, namely SP1.

In the Second World War, the estate was the site of gun emplacements, the golf course was mined - as previously mentioned

- and protective measures were placed along the coastline against the possibility of German invasion. Both Sir David and Lady Erskine had distinguished war careers, the latter serving as a Major with Field Marshall Montgomery, and being involved in the "D Day" campaign.

The present head of the family is Sir Peter Erskine, who inherited the title from his father Sir David who, sadly, died in 2007. Lady Catherine Erskine is an eminent gardener, and has built up a substantial snowdrops business. She has also been responsible for the regeneration of the estate's gardens which, in addition to taking part in the Scottish Gardens' Scheme, are open to the public on a daily basis. As a local, the author can, enthusiastically, recommend a visit to the estate gardens and surrounding walks.

Sir Peter, in addition to being a renowned photographer, has inherited, from 1976, from his father, the management of the estate. There are, currently, seventeen estate employees - having been more than 50 at the peak - involved both in the gardens and in the flourishing holiday letting business in the main estate house. The present house dates from 1879-81, having replaced the original building which was destroyed by fire. Sir Peter, in his excellent "Brief History of Cambo" – which is commended to the reader – charitably makes little of the fact that the fire took place during a "party" at a time when the family was away... Photographs of both the old and "new" houses are shown in Illustrations V and W.

Illustration V

Illustration W

The letting business was begun in the late 1940s, with students during the winter months, and holidaymakers in the summer months. The Erskines stopped letting to students in the mid 1990s, and have since invested heavily in upgrading the accommodation which is now available as holiday lets. Again, this author can highly recommend the accommodation which is currently available...which includes "working holidays" in the gardens - contact Lady Erskine for details.

Over the years, there have been numerous links between the estate and the village. The estate has been a regular employer of local people, although - in line with all country estates - on a smaller basis currently than hitherto. Local village enterprise has been supported, including the weaving business which flourished briefly in the 19th century. The Cambo Mains mill pond (established in 1860) - which can be seen from the main road just past the entrance to the Golf Links - was, in fact what was known as a "retting" pond, used to soak the fibre which was then made up into "Osnaburgh" fabric.

The estate has also been a significant benefactor to the village, contributing material to the church (referred to again later in this volume) in the form of communion cups, and more significantly, in the 1950s, the church organ – which had, originally been sited in the drawing room of Cambo House (again see Sir Peter Erskine's "Brief History"). The estate also took over, for a time, the funding of the local police presence in the village (from the Monypennys) until the costs became a state responsibility, and provided the land for the construction of the Memorial Hall which, as previously mentioned, remains the hub of the social activities of the village.

The Erskine family has also long been involved in local politics. Various family members have served on Fife Council, including Sir Thomas, Lady Magdalene, and Sir David and the current incumbent, Sir Peter remains heavily involved in local affairs through the Community Council, being its current Chair. Peter's father, Sir David Erskine, was Deputy Lord Lieutenant of the county, and its last non-socialist convenor. In this latter role, Sir David led the campaign, against the then prevailing government wisdom of the time, to have Fife retained as an administrative whole.

Thus, the Cambo Estate and the village have had close links over the centuries and, as the most notable landowner in the area, a pivotal role in the development of the parish. In conclusion, it might be noted that Sir Peter has recently announced that he intends to "extend... Cambo Estate's history of sympathetic and high standard improvements" by embarking on a plan to create a "truly unique global resort on the estate". It is hoped that such plans are given due consideration, and benefit both the Cambo Estate and the parish of Kingsbarns, in which it sits.

Summary

Although, by no means the only estate with links to the parish, it could be argued that Cambo has the widest range of past and ongoing contacts with the life of Kingsbarns. It is good to be able to observe that the current Erskine family are continuing in the entrepreneurial spirit of their forebears, and their efforts – in enabling the new golf course to be established, and in reviving an historic garden and house – are a credit to the village and wider parish.

Golf at Kingsbarns

There are several other references to golfing matters elsewhere in this volume - to the early establishment of a golfing society, to the mining of the then course during the war, and to the establishment of the "new" Kingsbarns Golf Links in 2000. Here we are going to go into greater detail on the subject of 'Golf at Kingsbarns'.

In fact, golf at Kingsbarns has a long, and distinguished history, dating back as far at least to 1793. In the Minutes of the neighbouring Crail Golfing Society of the 4th of September of that year, there is reference to the granting of permission to the members of the 'Kingsbarns Golfing Society' to play on the Crail links, and to wear their own uniform. This consisted of a blue jacket, compared with the red of Crail. The inference is that the Kingsbarns Golfing Society must have already been in existence prior to this date.

While it is, therefore, clear that there was a golfing society in existence at that time, the first formal record of the institution of the Club was in 1815, the Fife and Kinross Almanac of 1830 observing that "The Kingsbarns Golfing Society was instituted in 1815, and consists of almost forty, and as many Honorary members, in the list of whom it ranks several of the neighbouring proprietors, and nearly all of the respectable farmers in this and some of the neighbouring parishes. They meet regularly four times in the year to play golf viz., in February, May, August, and November." Even if it can't be proven that there was a club in existence prior to 1793, this early history still makes Kingsbarns the ninth oldest golf club in terms of establishment, a mere two places after Crail.

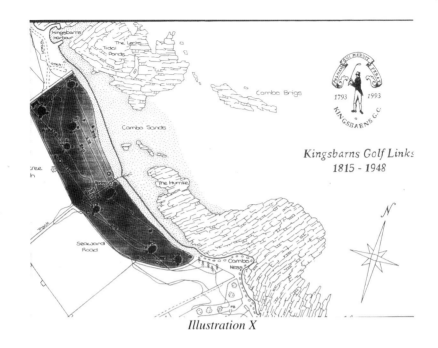

Kingsbarns Golf Links
1815 - 1948

Illustration X

Illustration X above shows the layout of the original nine hole links, reference on one of the club's trophies, the Erskine Cup, being to the granting of the use of the course to the Society in 1815 by Thomas, ninth Earl of Kellie. Earl Thomas also fitted up a large room in the village for the Society's quarterly meetings, and there is evidence that 'His Lordship' was entertained to dinner there in 1826. The first recorded medal, commissioned by the members themselves, is the 'Kingsbarns Golfing Society Silver Medal' of 1823, shown in Illustration Y, courtesy of its current owner, the renowned golf memorabilia collector, Peter Crabtree (a long standing member of the Royal and Ancient Golf Club of St Andrews). Mr. Crabtree, with other guests of honour, is pictured at the Golf Club's bicentenary dinner (in the later attached photograph). This particular medal bears the motto *"Palmam qui meruit ferat"*, which can be translated, literally, as "Let him who has won the palm bear it." This was the motto of Horatio, Lord, Nelson, and was widely adopted by various societies at that time.

Illustration Y

It would appear that, at around the time of the award of this first medal, the Society began to be known, instead, as Kingsbarns Golf Club. Certainly, a later medal to be gifted, by Captain W. H. Fielden, in 1841 (when he became Captain) is inscribed 'Club' rather than Society. The Fielden Gold Medal, at Illustration Z, was for competition amongst the members of every golfing society in Fife, its first winner, in June 1841, being Mr. Robert Haig of Seggie, an R&A member. Curiously, it was played again later in the same year, in November, and this latter month is when it was then played each year.

Illustration Z

Shortly after the establishment of the Fielden medal, (in 1844) a catastrophe befell the club when the tenant farmer on whose land it sat, one Mr. Duncan, carried out a threat which he had previously made, and ploughed up the course for farming. This event was followed shortly by the resignation, in 1846, of the Club's long serving Secretary, Alexander Latto. Mr Latto was also the schoolmaster of Kingsbarns school, and his burial place in the Church graveyard - shown in Illustration AA - is a splendid obelisk engraved with the legend "Erected by a few of his old scholars". Also, at Illustration AB, is a snuff box presented in 1831 to Mr. Latto in recognition 'of his gratuitous services as Secterary of the Club', again in the Peter Crabtree collection.

Illustration AA

Illustration AB

Whether precipitated by these events, it was not long before the original society/club was wound up. Most accounts adopt the date of the suspension of the operation of the club as being the 3rd. of August, 1849, this being repeated in a very informative article on the club in the October, 1908 issue of Golf Illustrated. The Club's Minutes of the 3rd. of August, 1849 resolved "to suspend, for a season, its future meetings". The meetings were adjourned 'sine die' after arranging for the collection of the medals from the various holders, and the appointment of a Committee "to inspect the Books, ascertain the state of the debts and notify to the different members the sums due…". While 1849 is the conventional - and almost certainly the correct date - for the suspension of the club's activities, it is interesting, however, to note that golf historian, Bobby Burnet, contests this account, saying that there are references in Farnie's golfer's Manual of 1862, that the club was still flourishing then, on its "…small and of sandy soil (links)". Whichever was the date for the dissolution of the club, it was resolved that the records and medals/cups would be preserved in the event of the club be revived at some future date.

This revival was, in fact, accomplished in 1922 when, at a public meeting in the Kingsbarns school, it was resolved to (re)form the Kingsbarns Golf Club. At that point, therefore, the nine hole course was reinstated, and a new clubhouse erected. This clubhouse is shown in Illustration AC, in the context of a childrens' competition held in 1934. By this time, golf was a more egalitarian pursuit than it had been in the early days, and the photograph shows how widespread was the interest in the sport amongst the local populace. Regular visitors to the village in the 1920s and 30s, Muriel and Doreen Anderson recall that the golf course was the most important part of their holidays, and the highlight the children's golf competition.

Illustration AC

The course was then suspended at the AGM on December 10th 1940, "owing to parts of the course being used for military purposes". Play was resumed after the December 1946 AGM, following a motion by John Y.Young, and seconded by R. W. Braid, with Bill Smith elected as Captain, and the then Headteacher, William W. Wilkie, re-elected as Secretary and Treasurer. However, within a year, it was decided to "give up the course", it being deemed that the club could not keep up the expenditure of its upkeep. It was decided, however, that the club should remain in existence - as it has since - with the various trophies played over Balcomie Links. Mr.Wilkie was, at that time, given a gold wristwatch, in recognition of his eighteen year stint as Secretary of the Golfing Society.

Since the Club's reinstatement, its egalitarian nature has continued and, although the membership is restricted to a maximum of fifty, its current membership comprises a wide range of professions and trades, as well as many retired gentlemen. All are proud to be members of such a venerable, and historic institution.

The golfing society having been re-established, there have been a number of further trophies created on behalf of the club, and these are shown in Illustration AD below, the trophies themselves being held, on loan, at the new Kingsbarns Golf Links, where they can be viewed. Comprising the Inglis Cup, Spence Cup and Sandeman medal, Erskine Cup and Wilson Medal, Cairns Cup and Cortorphine medal, and the Smith Cup, the competitions are still played over Balcomie Links – thus maintaining the much valued connections with the Crail Golfing Society, which have lasted over 215 years.

Kingsbarns Golf Club
TROPHIES

| Inglis Cup | Spence Cup | Erskine Cup |

| Cairns Cup | Duncan Cup | Turnbull Tankard |

| Wilson Medal | Sandeman Medal | Corstorphine Medal |

Illustration AD

Illustration AE also shows a medal from 1840 which recently came up for auction at Messrs. Lyon and Turnbull, making £17,000, and which is now reputed to be in the hands of a private collector. Whether its new owner will make the medal available for public view remains to be seen.

Illustration AE

The course itself, having not being permanently reinstated after the end of the Second World War, the few remaining member were co-opted into the Crail Golfing Society. While the course, therefore, had been 'lost' to the Second World War effort, it came to life again in 2000, with the establishment of the new Kingsbarns Golf Links (although not a club as such). A different "logo" was adopted for the new links, although the logic of its design is unknown, and can be seen in Illustration AF, which also shows the new layout of the course.

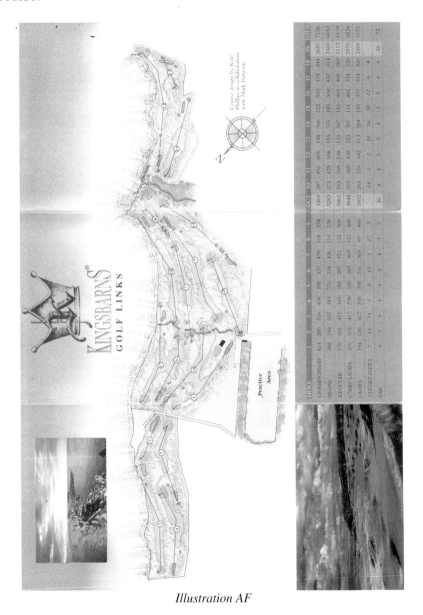

Illustration AF

The golf course has quickly attained championship status, now forming an integral part of the autumn Dunhill Links Championship, alongside The Old Course of St. Andrews, and Carnoustie. The Kingsbarns Golf Club itself remains in robust, good health as can be seen at Illustration AG, showing, (now) Sir Michael Bonallack, Peter Crabtree, Ron Stuart and other officials, at the bi-centenial dinner. The 2008 Captain, and former long time Secretary is Ron Stuart (far right in the picture), its Vice Captain is Len Phipps and the Secretary and Treasurer is Malcolm Lister.

Illustration AG

Living in Kingsbarns

As was emphasised at the end of the previous chapter, this text will deal mainly with life in Kingsbarns from the early 19th century onwards. The years encompassing the late 18th century and the beginnings of the 1800s were, of course, momentous for many communities in the UK, since they marked significant changes in employment patterns – with their resultant social impacts – from the industrial revolution which was sweeping through the country. As a predominantly rural community, Kingsbarns was affected much less than its urban counterparts, but there were still changes, both in the scale of the village population, and in the means of employment of its inhabitants.

The Reverend Beatson's Parish Account of 1791-7, for example, notes that, of the total population of 807, 467 resided in the village and the remaining 340 in the surrounding countryside. The rural nature of the parish at that time is abundantly clear, as not only would the "country" dwellers have predominantly been attached to the parish estates and farms, but many of the village inhabitants similarly so. The other main form of livelihood was fishing, supplemented by linen weaving in times of inclement weather. Beatson's successor, the long serving Reverend George Wright, reports in his account of 1834/5 that the population had increased to 1023 (from the 1831 Census), with 593 in the village and 430 in the country. Dr.Wright attributes the increase in the population to "the great improvement over the past fifty years in the science of agriculture, and to the extra and steady employment which the enclosing, draining, and extensive cultivation of waste lands has given." (Wright, 1835) It is noted in Wright's account that "….almost every family of the labouring classes keeps a sow; and its flesh, along with potatoes… and fish caught off the shore in summer, and herrings…salted in the neighbouring towns, with occasionally meat from the butcher, give an abundance of wholesome and nourishing food". (Wright, *Ibid.*)

Fishing would have developed beyond its subsistence status – as it had done at other East Neuk locations – had there been better harbour facilities at Kingsbarns. As early as 1758, the local fishermen reported that their harbour was "in a ruinous condition", and again in 1781 they petitioned for "some reparation on the pier…" (*ibid*). On each occasion they were granted only minimal assistance from the Heritors, and it was not until the mid 1850s that the harbour was extended. At that time, it was the initiative of a local farmer, John Duncan of Boghall who organised the construction of a second wall to enclose the harbour, his motivation being, not to enhance the capabilities of the fishing boats, but to create a base from which he could ship out his potato crops. The harbour gradually fell into disrepair and, by 1927, was "no longer viable". The general shape of the harbour area is still visible, particularly at low tide, but it has long since been an operational asset for the village.

The weaving, which families took on to supplement their incomes, was, of course, a cottage industry, conducted within their own homes. Dr.Wright, in his 1834/5 account remarks that "The kinds of cloth beside linen – which was also woven for their own use – which are wrought are called Osnaburgh and Dowlas." At the time of his writing there were thirty one looms in constant use in the village, and they provided a much needed source of income, particularly in the winter months when fishing was hazardous and unpredictable. It did not, however, provide a guaranteed level of supplementary income, Dr. Wright further remarking that the timing of his report had coincided with a slump in the weaving trade, such that it was providing a mere 1s. a day for the average family.

An interesting account of life in the parish at that time, is that covered by Karen Toon, in a privately published monograph in the collection of the St. Andrews University Library. In it, she notes that her father had been taken on (fee'd) as a farm worker, at North Quarter Farm – as was the custom at the time – at the St. Andrews Lammas Fair(or market). The family arrived at, and were collected from, Kingsbarns Station, to be taken to their farm quarters. Mrs Toon recalls the, then, still active harbour, with its catches of lobster and haddock, and remembers shopping in the various shops which then existed in the village.

As accounted by Mrs Toon's story – and from other accounts - during the course of the 19th century there was the development of other trades and ancilliary services in and around the village. These can be shown in the following list of occupations taken from the Parochial Directory for Fife and Kinross, 1861.

Blacksmiths

Anderson, George

Youlle, George

Boots and Shoemakers

Beatt, Dvaid

Doeg, Alexander

Johnstone George

Lothjian, Robert

Spence, Alexander

Carters

Brown, Alexander

Carmichael, James

Dressmakers

Anderson, Euphemia

Crawford, Margaret

Farmer. Ann

Forrester, Jean

Kay, Mrs. Mat

Lyall, Isabella

Monroe, Jesssie

Tailors

Corstorphine, William

Monepenny, W. T.

Reekie, James, Hillary

Rodger, William

Gardeners

Falconer, James

Melville, Robert

Grocers

Crighton D.(& spirits dealer)

Janice, Mary

Lawson, Christine

White, William

Wishart, Elizabeth (& Temperance Refreshment Rooms)

Joiners and Wrights

Gillespie, James

Scott, James

Scott, Laurance

Some families thus had established a varied range of trades, again often as a supplement to other forms of income, while service businesses such as blacksmiths and retail outlets were also set up to cater for the parish's growing population and its work related and other needs. At the peak, the village could boast of several shops, including a draper's, two grocery shops, two 'sweetie' shops, and two public houses with, for a time, a local fish and chip shop as well. Most of the shops were on main Street, between the Square and Lady Wynd, but there were two incorporated into houses, one in Wellgate(Aggie Kay's) in the Square, and another in the Pleasaunce in what is now known as Station Road.

As previously mentioned, one of the pubs was housed in the Cambo Arms (seen at Illustration AH), as in Pevsner described as "housed in a plain but attractive early 19th century coaching inn" – with facilities for tying up horses well into the 1960. Having been run by the Stewarts for many years, the Cambo Arms was taken over by the Fraser family in 1990s and continued in uninterrupted service from its early establishment until 2002, when it was deemed that there was insufficient local business to justify its existence. To the relief of the author, and, no doubt, many other locals, after a period when it was closed as a public house, the Cambo Arms was resurrected, in 2004 as the somewhat curiously renamed "Barns at Kingsbarns" and, despite having again changed hands (and again…) is still trading as the village pub. The late Isobel Stewart had many memories of her time as the pub landlady, not least its part in village life. There were regular village activities, centred on the Cambo Arms, including weddings, and the associated 'stag nights', including one of John

Robb, who had his feet painted with gentian violet – welcome back such innocent times..

Illustration AH

At that time, the pub was also a supplier of petrol to locals and visitors alike, with Mrs. Stewart leaving her bar duties (with customers taking over !) to serve cars, vans and lorries. Eventually, it became uneconomic to continue the 'service station' activities although, apparently, the tanks are still there under the forecourt of the pub.

It is clear that the village shops and, no doubt, the pubs benefitted from trade from the growing, indigenous population as well as seasonal tourist business. Kingsbarns has never been a tourist 'Mecca' to the extent of Crail or Anstruther, but there must have been sufficient tourist trade to help sustain the local economy, including shops and licensed premises. One interesting piece of evidence that local traders did aim at the tourist trade is that a, regrettably unknown entrepreneur developed a Kingsbarns "crest" which was transfer printed on to china items made elsewhere in Fife (probably Kirkaldy). A representation of this crest is shown in Illustration AI, and is taken from a piece of china still in the possession of a current descendant of a family which lived in and around the village through several generations. It is the intention to include this item in the permanent archive of Kingsbarns related material.

Illustration AI

It is further interesting that, in choosing to create a new crest or "logo" for the current Kingsbarns Golf Links, no reference was made to the, admittedly "manufactured" crest which had been used on Kingsbarns souvenir china for at least the previous century. It is fair to say that it has no clear historical connection to either the older golfing societies/clubs or, indeed, to the village itself.

Over the past half century, the village shops have fared less well, in line with other rural communities with falling populations. Although many long time residents such as Bill and Mary Swan can recall the bustle of the local retail trade – including the sweetie shops…, even as relatively "recent" as 1952, writers such as Alex Smith were bemoaning the fact that not one of the indigenous trades was left in the village, that the "shops have been reduced from three to one over the past forty years" and that "….the only tradesmen's premises are (now) those of two blacksmiths and one joiner, employing six men in total.". There had, in fact, been three blacksmiths in the village at one time – two being on the recently renamed "Smiddy Burn" but, of course, there are none now.

As for the village shops, there remains a local sub-post office and local shop, currently owned and run by Len and Sandra Phipps. Particularly given the ageing nature of the village population, the shop - and post office - is a vital lifeline for the local community and yet the post office has been still under threat of closure as a result of national Post Office cutbacks. At the time of writing, this situation remains unresolved, although the post office has escaped the latest set of cutbacks...

One interesting story relating to the post office is that of the 'new' postbox, which was installed in 1991. The then, enterprising Postmaster, Ken Crichton, had established that there were several of the original Victorian Penfold pillar box moulds left in existence, and wrote to the Post Office authorities in Dundee to ask if one would be available for the village. Amazingly, the last one had been rejected by the descendants of the author, Robert Louis Stevenson, and so was available for installation in the village. This was arranged to happen at a ceremony organised by the Community Council, and took place on 12th. July 1991. Local schoolchildren were dressed in period costume for the event, and the former postmistress, Mrs. Common, was also present (see Illustrations AJ and AK showing both Ken Crichton and Mrs Common respectively).

Illustration AJ

Illustration AK

A more detailed account of the development of the village school is covered later in this publication, but here it is worth noting that the school role was as high as 118 in the early 1900s, but is now only in the 20s. A new Head was recently appointed (Cameron Watson) and the school remains an important link with the past history of the village and, indeed, as the foundation of its future. The trend remains for "graduates" of the village primary school to go on to, either, Madras College in St. Andrews, or Waid Academy in Anstruther, thus preserving local links. It is, however, an unfortunate fact that the lack of local employment prospects means that a growing proportion of the then secondary school leavers have to leave the district to seek careers elsewhere.

Until the 1980s, there was a permanent police presence in the village. Various houses have been used as the Police Station, and residence of the local "Bobbie", including two on Seagate. One of these earlier premises is pictured at Illustration AL, the policeman's family eventually being provided with new premises on Smiddy Burn. Life for the local "bobby" was no sinecure, duties extending way beyond any concept of "9 to 5". It is still pertinent to observe that the monitoring of village life, particularly the evening activities of some of the younger inhabitants, would be better served were there still a permanent police presence…This comment is made, not to reflect the fact that Kingsbarns is a "hotbed" of social trouble – it is not. Rather, it represents a more general social "problem", that of police forces across the country trying to cover extensive rural and semi-rural areas with insufficient resources.

Illustration AL

Various local institutions, including those linked to the church, and to be covered later, have remained the bedrock of the social life of the village. These would include the ongoing Womens' Rural Institute (WRI), the Ladies' Work Party (covered elsewhere), the mens' and youth social groups (alas, no longer ongoing), and annual - and periodic - social events such as fairs and the annual flower show. Now in its 93rd year, the Annual Flower Show is still going strong, with long serving residents such as Mrs. Mary Frail - belittling her name - and Ron and Isobel Stuart, continuing in the "winners' enclosure" across a wide variety of prize categories. John Bell, father of Margaret and Jean Bell, is also shown in Illustration AM, accepting one of his many prizes at the Flower Show over the years. Another notable regular winner was Bob Rodger, whose onions were of sufficient fame that they gained him a place in the Guinness Book of Records…Bill Greig also remembers the annual sports/'highland games', in which professionals competed, covering such events as tossing the caber, cycle races, highland dances, and horse parades - and even a 'married womens' race'... (see Illustration AN below).

Illustration AM

Illustration AN

In the formative period of the village's economic development, transport communications were vital. A crucial factor in this respect was the railway connection on the coastal line which linked

Kingsbarns to the Anstruther line, first to Boarhills in 1883 and then to St. Andrews in 1887. While the "local" station was some distance from the village, the railway line served the local populace from its establishment to its closure, as a passenger station, in the early 1930s. The railway line remained open, for freight traffic, until 1965, a poignant photograph showing its last day of operation, and it remained the first station from St. Andrews to have a double track, as can be seen in Illustration AO below.

Illustration AO

There is an interesting vignette of the continuing operation of the station during the Second World War. The then stationmaster (Mr. Smith) was left short staffed when his signalman was called up for active service, and his wife, Alison, was then "appointed" as assistant to her husband stationmaster and, having passed her "tests", was required to help run the station until the end of the war. An account in the Citizen of 23rd January, 1943, reports Mrs. Smith as emphasising that she had to juggle her domestic duties with the requirements of the job, but she was not averse to requiring her husband to share the kitchen chores when necessary – a welcome sign of early "womens' lib" in the area. Mrs. Smith's talents, in fact, were of sufficient interest to the public at large that she was interviewed by Women's Hour on BBC radio.

Since the demise of the railway, Kingsbarns residents have relied on local bus services, which - it must be said - have provided a regular service for the increasing number of people who have found it necessary to seek employment outside the village itself. Even so, one local resident reports that, even with recent improvements to the local bus services, his daily commute to work in Dundee still takes one and a half hours each way (just a little better than compared to the previous two hours).

Post War life in the Parish

The end of WW2 marked a watershed for social development in much of the UK, Kingsbarns not being remotely exempted from such factors. The two major trends, in social terms, have been the progressive departure of young people from the village - seeking employment elsewhere - and the similarly, progressive, ageing of the remaining population.

The fairly recent development of note mentioned earlier has, of course, been the construction of a new golf course to replace the former links which were mined during WW2. A separate account of "Golf at Kingsbarns" is detailed within its own chapter in the book. At this point, it is pertinent to note that its construction has been a mixed blessing for the village. An extremely enterprising former pupil of Crail Primary School, Paul Rennie (whose work will form part of the permanent Kingsbarns archive) canvassed opinion from local residents on the, then, proposed "new" golf course – among other matters – and it was clear, from the various responses that it was hoped that the "Kingsbarns Golf Links" would bring business to the village in the form of jobs and increased trade for the local shop.

There is no doubt that the golf course has put the village name "on the map". It comprises one of three courses used for the Dunhill

Links Championship, now a constituent part of the European PGA Tour events and, as such, is subject to international recognition. It is also now an integral part of the Fife golf "tour" for many international visitors. Indeed, the author's own elder daughter, who manages a restaurant in Houston, Texas, has come across several visitors who have "played Kingsbarns", however, the pecuniary effects of the reopening of the links have not been particularly significant. Most visitors to the course arrive by car/bus – or helicopter! – and make no contact with the village itself. The shop has occasional periods of extra business, particularly at the time of the Dunhill Links Championship, but otherwise the existence of the new golf links has had comparatively little impact on the village economy.

It is no criticism of the developers of the new Kingsbarns Golf Links – whose brief was not to create local employment - but it is a fact that relatively few new, permanent jobs have been created as a result of its reopening. Stuart McEwan, the General Manager of the Golf Links, also acknowledges that the experience of playing the course leaves little, if any, impression of the parish community in which the golf course sits. The construction of the course has also taken away from the villagers, land which was, formerly, part of their 'Sunday walks.' It has also made the Coastal Path - an integral right of both locals and visitors, a more hazardous process. While there are, thus, mixed opinions on the golf course, however, the author feels compelled to acknowledge the role played by a long time resident, Lord Taylor of Gryff, whose widow is still an important local inhabitant. Lord Taylor was one the foremost local 'movers' for the reconstruction of the golf course, and it is fair to say that his efforts were extremely significant in bringing the project to fruition.

An account of the village - and parish – since the end of WW2 - therefore has to acknowledge that it is of a community which, at best, is in a period of consolidation, and, at worse, is in decline. There remains a good community spirit in the village. The WRI and the Annual Flower Show go on in strength, while the Community Council - ably supported by local councillors - continues to deal with local issues. There are also several families who maintain their historical links with the parish – including the Dicks, Ritchies, Hutchisons and Swans, some of whose younger generations still reside in the village.

Summary

This section of the text has sought to set out the social changes which have affected village life over the period since the early 1800s. There is no doubt that the village has been influenced by the urbanisation of society, with more and more young people having to seek employment elsewhere, a trend exacerbated by the rise of property prices to levels which young locals can ill afford. However, there remains a good spirit of community in Kingsbarns, evidenced not least by the regular, various village activities such as the recently held 'Secret Gardens of Kingsbarns' event on the weekend of 29th July, 2008 and, as shown in Illustration AP, the even more recent 2008 Flower Show, again pictured.

Illustration AP

Final Conclusions

The history of Kingsbarns has been a story which has 'needed telling' for a long time. The author is, therefore, proud and honoured to have been part of the team which has now brought the project to fruition. At the outset, it was stated that it was not the intention to write an academic tome on the subject, rather it was hoped that we could produce a volume which would cover the key elements of the history of the village and its outlying areas, and of the experiences of those living in Kingsbarns now and in the past.

It was necessary, however, to set the scene with an account of the early history of the village, and of the characteristics of the interesting, and historically important, buildings and houses therein. That having been done, the remainder of the book has been about social issues concerning Kingsbarns' residents past and present. Thus, there was a chapter on the formation of the church and school, their intertwined histories, with memories of school pupils both in the recent past, and in more distant times. Thus, there was an account of the impact of both World Wars on the village, and the surrounding farms - with a significant feature on the story of the sinking, off Kingsbarns, of HMS Success in 1914. This was followed by a 'short history' of the Cambo Estate - relying heavily on Sir Peter Erskine's volume of the same name - and of the very close relationship between estate and village over many centuries.

The volume would not have been complete without reference to 'golf at Kingsbarns', given that the Golf Club (formerly Golfing Society) is the ninth oldest club in existence. However, while one hopes that historical accuracy has been observed, the account here has again been broadened to include how golf has affected the village, not least as a tourist attraction in the inter-war years.

The final, main section of the volume was then 'living in Kingsbarns', linked with the memories of current residents, and of villagers, alas, no longer with us. Thus, that chapter dealt with the changing population numbers - and occupations - over the period since the early 1800s. In particular, it focussed on the social changes in the post-war period, and how these have affected Kingsbarns and its residents. It was these social changes - particularly an ageing population, declining local employment opportunities for young people, and rising property prices facing those who wished to remain in the area - which has prompted the Community Council, in recent years, to assess the future outlook for the village.

The first of these initiatives was a commission to St. Andrews University, organised by Claire Wright and Sir Peter Erskine, then Chair and Community Councillor respectively, to construct scenarios of the village's future. Two such scenarios were produced, one optimistic in the sense of an increasing housing stock in the village, helping to support the school, shop and inn; the other predicting a gradual decline in the village as a viable social unit.

Subsequently, under the Chairmanship of Joyce Taylor, the Community Council authorised a study amongst the village populace as to which direction Kingsbarns should take. The purpose of this study was to make clear to Fife Council the views of the villagers as to the optimal future of the community. Material pertaining to this survey will be available in the forthcoming archive. Suffice to say, at this juncture, the results pointed strongly to limited future housing development in the village, a conclusion supported by over 50% of those surveyed.

Finally, the author would like to point to an optimistic future for the village, balancing the needs of local landowners with the interests of the wider community. It is hoped that such a positive future is in store for Kingsbarns, with a viable school, a local shop and post office, a community inn, and a continuing and new group of families taking the village forward into the future.

Chats with Villagers – Past and Present

A Chat with Mary Frail

Having arrived in the village in 1954, and having lived continuously in Kingsbarns since then, Mary Frail can remember lots of interesting tales about village life. In the photograph above, she is shown with her daughter Alice, probably taken not long after her arrival. While there are further references to Mary's experiences in the village over the years in which she has lived here in the chapter on "Living in Kingsbarns", this account goes further in relating her time in the village. It is, primarily, based on the interview with Mary at her home, conducted by Jean Bell, and supplemented by a further 'chat' with the author.

As regards transport to the village, one of Mary's early recollections is of cattle arriving by train - as well as people - and having to be walked to Kingsbarns Farm on what was then an unfenced and unmarked road. She also recalls walking cattle to grazing pastures, some way from the farms. There were then three farms within the village - Kingsbarns, North Quarter, and South Quarter - all of which were both dairy and arable in nature. Transported by the railway were the important farm products of potatoes - to 'down south' - and sugar beet, to the plant in Cupar. Serving these farms were two 'portable' mills, which were taken to site as required. Horses on the farms (and at Cambo) were a common sight until the late 1950s and Mary remembers horses at Kingsbarns Farm until even the mid-sixties.

Petrol was available from pumps at the Cambo Arms from the 1930s, although motorised visitors were uncommon until the 1960s. This did not prevent regular visits from holidaymakers, travelling mostly to the village by bus, and staying at one of the several houses – as well as the Cambo Arms - which offered accommodation. Mary remembers a number of such holiday lets/ B & Bs, for example Polly Gillespie in North Street, Mrs. MacDonald in Seagate, Miss Lyall in Bell's Wynd, and the Hills in Lady Wynd. It is in the light of changing holiday patterns that the village can now only list a few such holiday accommodations - the (thankfully reopened) Cambo Arms- under its new name - and a cottage in Lady Wynd, amongst others in the new steading developments

One of the significant occupations of the Frails was the operation of the travelling chip shop, which they took over from the Nichol family. The Nichols had established a chip shop at the corner of Main Street and Lady Wynd, Mrs. Nichol's mother Mrs. Wishart having originally cooked the fare in a converted wash boiler (!). The Nichols also had a kiosk/van at the beach for teas and sweets, and it was this vehicle which Mary's husband, Hugh acquired, and converted it into a travelling chip van. This van travelled as far and wide as Cameron, Peat Inn, and Largoward, before being replaced by a caravan which was parked in a back garden of Cottage Row. Villagers and visitors enjoyed their fish and chips from the chip van until, eventually, it ceased trading in the late 60s/early 70s.

The other abiding memory of Mrs. Frail is the sense of community in the village. While not unusual in rural villages of the time, Kingsbarns could boast of a wide range of village activities, right up to the 1970s. There were, for example, regular dances held in the school hall before the opening of the Memorial Hall, with Mr. Nicol playing the accordion. There were regular whist drives – with up to 25 tables - raising funds for local causes such as the boy scouts, and Jumble Sales which served similar ventures. There was the annual Flower Show - in which Mary has been a perennial winner - referred to elsewhere in this volume - as is the Ladies Work Party, and the one off celebrations for the present Queen's Coronation in 1953, in which there was the then rare treat of TV in the 'old hall', combined with a fancy dress parade.

Overall, Mary Frail has enjoyed a fulfilling life in Kingsbarns, while regretting the passing of the ways of so many local customs. She remains upbeat, however, about the spirit of the village to forge a unified existence into the 21st century.

The Memories of Nona Robb

Nona was born in a house in the Square, Kingsbarns, the second youngest of a family (the Hutchisons) which can trace its lineage in the village back to her great grandmother's birth in 1826. The family house, occupied at least back to her great-grandparents' time, is now known as Cessneuk, although Nona has no recollection of it having such a name - or any name for that matter - during her family's period of residence. The house, covered in the 'Scene Setting' chapter, is a late 18th century building, possibly originally of single storey construction, with additional storeys - and an external staircase - being added later.

Nona started at Kingsbarns School on the 13th of April 1942, when she was just short of her fifth birthday. She recalls that, at that time, there were three classes and, therefore, three teachers, including the Headmaster, Mr.Wilkie. The classes were made up of children of different ages, primarily grouped as 'infant', 'middle', and 'older/advanced', which ended with the Qualifying Exam, and transfer to secondary school.

In those days, all of the children of the village played together, and were allowed to play in the school playground in the evenings, rounders being a popular game. A further game of note was that of hopscotch, sometimes called in Scotland, 'peevers', but in Kingsbarns known as 'poldies'. In this local version, the most prized peever/poldie was, most often or not, replaced with a more modest boot polish tin, sufficiently weighted with pebbles and stones to allow it to be pushed out and then 'hopped' back to 'home' in fine style. Games were seasonal, with skipping ropes and balls used to carry out traditional routines, often to the accompaniment of chants or songs. The highlight of the winter season was, of course, Christmas, when the tree provided by Kippo Farm was decorated by the local children, who then put on a performance to celebrate the event.

Nona's early childhood coincided with the Second World War, a testing time for all communities, both rural and urban. While too young to appreciate the enormities of these events, she can recall discussions amongst the family about such as the D Day Landings, and was aware of the disruptions to local life in this part of North East Fife. These would have included the Crail and Dunino Airfields, the presence of Italian Prisoners of War, and Polish soldiers billeted in the area. Life in the war years, however, does not have any particularly grim memories for Nona, however, as her recollections are of a family with a large garden, with chickens reared, and ample ground for vegetable cultivation. Given such ability to produce one's own food, Nona's view, in retrospect, is that rural communities such as Kingsbarns, may have fared less badly in this respect than many urban areas.

Nona's wartime (and thereafter) memories also include other favourable aspects, such as the Christmas parties at Crail Airfield - where her father worked - and trips, in the immediate post-war years, to the cinema at the Kilduncan camp associated with the Dunino Airfield. There were, at that time, still Polish personnel based at Dunino, several of whom married local girls. One of these was Martin Cerajewski, who married local girl, Amy Braid, and who then lived for a considerable period in the village. It is interesting to note that there is historical continuity to this relationship in that Martin's son, Len, still fires the gun, on Hogmanay, to signify the bringing in of the 'New Year'.

In her later childhood, Nona was a member of the Brownies and then the Guides, run by the formidable Lady Erskine. Nona remembers outings to Cambo Estate, where there was a pond which was later converted into a present tennis court, and also recalls that there was, on the estate, a house, child-sized and fitted-out, which the children loved. Nona's family moved to Seagate in 1953, when new housing was constructed, the attached photograph being taken during that time, and has been in her present home (at No 21) since 1968. Her family has grown, and prospered since then, and she remains a valued and symbolic member of the community.

Note :

The material used in this section on Nona's memories of life in the village is, primarily, based on an interview conducted by Kit McMahon and Dorothy Cameron, supplemented by a further 'chat' with the author.

Memories with Bill Swan

Bill was born in his present home, Rowan Cottage on Seagate, in 1917, but can trace his connections to the village at least back to his maternal great-grandfather. Bill is the oldest resident of Kingsbarns whose origins begin in the village, an honour which he has described, to the author, as being somewhat 'double-edged'…The material for these recollections, in mainly based on an interview conducted by Cala Cobb, and supplemented by a discussion with Bill by the author.

The present family house is, by no means the only property owned over time by the Swans in the village. His great-grandfather had, originally, lived in Lady Wynd, adjacent to the location of his joiner father's workshop. The family also owned, amongst others, the house on Back Stile now known as 'Greenloaning' - although in those days called 'Seaview'. At that time Bill's paternal grandfather was clerk of works for the architect, Robert (later Sir) Lorimer, who was then working on the extension of 1884 of Cambo House which Pevsner describes as having a "balustraded clock tower".

Schooling was, for Bill, up to the age of 11, the village primary, and he is shown with some classmates in the accompanying photograph. His family then emigrated to Australia, but stayed only some three years, and so his further education was completed back in Scotland. There are abiding memories of the village in Bill's early childhood, such as 'THE' shop in Kingsbarns, Aggie Kay's grocery shop in the square - described by Bill as the Kingsbarns' 'Asda', and the two sweetie shops in Main Square and in the Pleasaunce.

In addition to the village shops, Bill recalls that, even into more recent times, milk could be obtained from any of the three farms, while Kingsbarns was also served by vehicles, horse-drawn and later mechanised, selling meat, fish, cakes and fruit and vegetables. In some ways, it seemed that such a rural community as Kingsbarns was, at least, as well served for provisions as in the present supermarket dominated days.

There was an interesting event involving Bill, at the advent of the new Millenium, which takes his family history connections with the village history back full circle. It had been considered that an appropriate marking of the new century, in relation to the school, would be the reinstatement of the long-defunct bell - to mark the start, and closing of the school day. Funding for the reinstatement of the bell tower - the old one having been deemed to be unsafe - remained an issue until Kingsbarns Golf Links Limited, the operators of the new golf course, generously put up the required monies. Since it had been Bill's father who had made the original cupola for the bell, it was entirely natural that he should unveil the new awning, the issue previously covered in the chapter on "Church and School" (Illustration L).

Bill has recently had his 91st birthday in the village and he and his wife Mary (who was a teacher at Kingsbarns School from Sept 1936 to Spring 1939) - and photographed here together - remain integral to the social life of the village, and to its links with the past.

The Recollections of Ian Turnbull

Ian's recollections include the acquisition of the farm, Boghall, by his grandparents. Thus, by the end of the Second World War, the Turnbulls were in charge of Boghall Farm, Ian being the continuity between the generations from his uncles and cousins. He is here also photographed at the presentation in the Memorial Hall to the retiring Post-Mistress Mrs Rachel Brown, emphasising his role in village and community life.

In the farming communities horse power remained necessary well into the 1950s, one pair to 50 arable acres being deemed necessary. One ploughman worked and cared for his two horses and their harnesses, with the horses used to plough, pull implements - binders, threshers, harrows, mowers, potato diggers, and carts.

Crop rotation was in a six pattern cycle, oats, potatoes, wheat, turnips, barley and hay. The potatoes were harvested by hand, with a school holiday granted in October for the children to earn extra money for winter clothing , boots or bikes .The Turnbulls did not breed their own cattle, but bought in Irish cattle from Glasgow markets to fatten for the last six months. These were then sold to local butchers, who prepared them for market.

Agricultural workers were contracted for a year, the terms of which could be extended for an additional year at the Lammas Market, primarily negotiated at the Royal Hotel in South Street. Such arrangements have become significantly different in the years since the Second World War, however, with farm labourers being hired on a normal contractual basis. Ian's farming operations have continued, however, on a mix of arable and dairy basis, and farming remains a constituent part of the Kingsbarns economy.

Note:

These notes are based on material gathered from an interview with Cala Cobb.

It is with particular regret that this book was not published sooner, as Ian sadly passed away in December 2008 after a long illness. Our heartfelt thanks go to him for his input to both this book and to the community in general.

Chats From The Past –Ann Common

During the course of the project group's researches, an account of an interview with Ann Common was found, dating most probably from the early to mid 1980s, dealing with her life in the village. The author has, therefore, utilised this material on the basis that it represents a Chat from the Past.

Mrs. Common was the Postmistress in the village of Kingsbarns from 1941 until 1952, and clearly had lots of interesting memories of times during that period, but also both before and after. She is shown, as a much older lady, in the earlier picture of the unveiling of the 'new' post-box in 1988, and also here in another charming family photograph in the back garden of the Post Office.

One early memory is of the houses using paraffin lamps, because electricity did no reach the village until 1933. The few street lamps also burned paraffin, and Mrs. Common recalls the lamplighters having great difficulty in lighting them in windy weather..! There was no mains water supply until shortly after the Second World War, moreover, hence most householders were dependent on their own wells, or had to use the 'fountain' in the village square. Mrs. Common has a recollection of the water from the pump in the square tasting 'different' – but does not say whether she thought to be better or worse than that from the other pumps…

The memories go back to before 1930, since that was the year the railway station closed to passenger traffic. Mrs. Common comments that "trains ran regularly between St. Andrews and Leven carrying passengers and goods". She goes on to comment that "Entering the village fom the Station Road, the busy Smiddy was the first building sighted and it was possible to watch the blacksmith (Mr. Brown) shoeing horses and enjoy the flare of the fire."

"The next house was occupied by another 'Mr Brown' and, apparently, to distinguish him – since he owned a (rare) motor car for hire , he was known as "Coachy Brown". Other residents of Station Road (at one time called 'Kippo Loan') were the Misses Scott, Miss Lothian and, in Torrie House, the McLarens. Across from Station Road, "the Church seems outwardly much the same today (ie. at the time of this interview) as it was in 1931." Inside, the main difference was the pipe organ in one of the galleries, replacing the small organ which stood below the pulpit.

Mrs. Common comments on various other houses in the Square, including the Schoolhouse – in which Mr. Wilkie and family lived. Kingsbarns House gets a mention with a little story of how the then resident, Miss Todd, used to call her garden 'The New Forest', on account of the number of new trees which had been planted. The Hutchisons' Cessneuk is also covered, with mention of the tale of it having been, at one time, the base for a smuggling operation - a story subject to much local speculation over the years.

The memories then move on to Cessneuk's neighbour, the house in which stood 'Miss Kay's shop. To quote Mrs. Common, "It is difficult to convey to anyone the exact appearance and atmosphere inside Miss Kay's shop. It had a stone floor, and a counter on each side as customers entered. Behind one counter was the stock of drapery goods; behind the other was the stock of groceries, sweets and tobacco. Miss Kay used a large sharp knife for cutting ham and bacon. Since the shop also sold paraffin, she can remember how the smell of the paraffin mingled with the groceries and drapery goods and, although oil lamps were used when darkness fell "how dim it was".

Curiously, these memories do not extend, directly, to her own time as Postmistress, those experiences not being mentioned at all. However, with these notes, Mrs.Common has given us a vivid - and evocative - picture of life in the village over a period spanning some fifty years.

A Talk with Andy Sherriff

The photograph above is of a young Andy in his Aunt Chrissy's garden with her rather impressive cat.

Andy's shared reminiscences of village life are drawn from the history of generations of his mother's family, the Martins who originate from Falkland, his father's family who lived and worked in and around the village, and his own fond memories. The family grave in the churchyard bears their names. He retains many old photographs, letters, maps and mementoes in his own personal collection; some appear elsewhere in this book. Andy's parents, Andrew and Margaret Sherriff, married during WW2 then suffered immediate separation, as many others did. His father was captured near Dunkirk shortly afterwards, and spent the remaining war years as a POW in Poland.

Born after the war, Andy and his younger brother Jim spent their childhood at Retreat Cottage, along with his grandparents until 1948, where he recalls life there without the conveniences of modern living. The village survived without piped water to the houses until the 1950s. Householders had to carry water from pumps and wells that were scattered around the village; some still exist hidden in private gardens. In this context, a particular memory emerges of procedures at the smaller drinking establishment, known as "The Auld Hoose" in Main Street. Without running water on the premises, an agreement existed whereby someone from the pub would cross the road, to Rosebank Cottage, to fetch buckets of water to "swill" the glasses. Photograph evidence appears in the book to show the "Auld Hoose" with an outside wall that served to screen the outside roofless lavatory from public view. When the piped water eventually arrived, Andy's home along with most others in the village was modernized to a much higher standard with better kitchen and bathroom facilities. Andy's home had electricity, but only one socket as he recalls. The momentous arrival of the "Baby Belling" cooker sticks vividly in his memory. He also remembers the village's first television set, in a house on Seagate where village children would congregate to watch. In 1953 he watched the queen's coronation on a TV located in the village hall. He recalls this TV set as being home-made and with a magnifying screen in front of it to boost the picture size.

Andy tells of an interesting account, drawn from old photographs, of a disastrous event when, in the process of extensive digging work in the village, the main drains became inadvertently filled in resulting in the flooding of Main Street, The Square and Station Road. Photographic records elsewhere in this book show the result of this incident. Such events were balanced later by further successful digging to install underground electricity and telegraph lines which, to this day, is an attractive feature of the village, now free from overhead cables. Again, photographs appear in this book to highlight these features and also the old paraffin street lights which, Andy recalls, after removal for upgrade, were stored in the old village

Barracks building before being taken to the dump near the beach to be crushed and buried.

Andy recalls that the village was never without opportunities for a social life, having several highlights to the year. One such example was the annual Flower Shows, which were always succeeded by a very popular "Dance" evening. Other villagers have recalled the popularity of regular dances that were held in the Memorial Hall in the village which attracted people from far and wide. Other memories abound of the Youth Club in the 1960s at the school, of Sports Days and other games (Quoits, Tossing the Caber etc) held in the field adjacent to the Manse.

Overall, Andy's story paints a picture of someone with a strong sense of personal and social history, derived from his close family ties, personal memories and his large archive material (copies of which he has kindly offered to be stored in the village history archive).

Note:

These notes are based on material gathered from an interview with Kit McMahon.

Selected Bibliography

Baird, Bob., Shipwrecks of the Forth and Tay, 2009, Whittles publishing.

Cook, H., Scots Magazine, January, 2002, article on the wrecking of H.M.S Success.

Crail Church Through the Centuries, Crail Parish Church, 1999.

Erskine, Sir Peter, A Brief History of Cambo, Cambo House, undated.

Fife and Kinross, Parochial Directory, 1861.

Fife, Malcolm, Crail and Dunino The Story of Two Scottish Airfields, 2003, GMS Enterprises, Peterborough.

Stansfield, G., Fife's Lost Railways, Stenlake Publishing, Catrine, 1998.

Golf Illustrated, October, 1908.

Kingdom Magazine, Autumn 2003, article on the Kilduncan Stone.

Kingsbarns Parish Accounts, various dates included.

Kingsbarns Kirk Session Minutes, held at St. Andrews University Library

Kingsbarns Heritors' Minutes, held at Register House, Edinburgh

Kingsbarns School Log, held at Fife county Archive, Markinch

Kingsbarns School Board Minutes, held at Fife County Archive, Markinch

Lamont-Brown, R., Fife and History and Legend, 2002, John Donald, Edinburgh.

Leighton, J. M., History of the County of Fife, Glasgow, Joseph Swan, 1840.

Millar. A.H., Fife; Pictorial and Historical, Cupar, A. Westwood & Son, 1895.

Pevsner's "The Buildings of Scotland", Fife Volume, by John Gifford, 1988.

Smith, A. T., Railway Walking, Kingdom Promotions, Elie.

'The Citizen', various issues cited.

Toon, Karen, "Memories of Life in Kingsbarns", privately published, held at St. Andrews University Library.

Wood, Harry. B, Golfing Curios and the Like, London, Sherratt and Hughes, 1910.

The following list details the Illustrations within the text of the main chapters of this book and their suppliers.

Illustration A	-	www.Scran.ac.uk
Illustration B	-	Postcard, George Sutherland
Illustration C	-	Society of Antiquaries of Scotland Vol 35 (2005)
Illustration D	-	Tayside & Fife Archeological Journal Vol 7 (2001)
Illustration E	-	Unknown
Illustration F	-	www.197aerial.co.uk
Illustration G	-	Ian Somerville, Kingsbarns
Illustration H	-	Kingsbarns Hall committee

Illustration I	-	www.197aerial.co.uk
Illustration J	-	University of St Andrews Library, Ref: ALB5-29
Illustration K	-	Kingsbarns Millenium committee
Illustration L	-	Kingsbarns Primary school
Illustration M	-	Margaret Thomas, Leven
Illustration N	-	Jean Bell, Kingsbarns
Illustration O	-	Margaret Thomas, Leven (www.cwgc.org.uk)
Illustration P	-	www.hazegray.org.uk
Illustration Q	-	Jean Bell, Kingsbarns
Illustration R	-	Andy Sherriff, Anstruther
Illustration S	-	Andy Sherriff, Anstruther
Illustration T	-	Andy Sherriff, Anstruther
Illustration U	-	Jean Bell, Kingsbarns
Illustration V	-	Dowager, Lady Erskine
Illustration W	-	Dowager, Lady Erskine
Illustration X	-	Unknown
Illustration Y	-	Peter Crabtree (alexmyers.co.uk)
Illustration Z	-	Peter Crabtree
Illustration AA	-	Jean Bell, Kingsbarns
Illustration AB	-	Peter Crabtree (alexmyers.co.uk)
Illustration AC	-	Messrs Pettigrew / Waterston (nee Anderson), Glasgow
Illustration AD	-	Ron Stewart, Kingsbarns Golf Club
Illustration AE	-	Lyon and Turnbull
Illustration AF	-	Tourist Office, St Andrews
Illustration AG	-	Unknown
Illustration AH	-	Postcard, George Sutherland
Illustration AI	-	Andy Sherriff, Anstruther
Illustration AJ	-	Ken Crichton, Kingsbarns
Illustration AK	-	Ken Crichton, Kingsbarns
Illustration AL	-	www.Scran.ac.uk
Illustration AM	-	Jean Bell, Kingsbarns
Illustration AN	-	Mary Harris, Leuchars
Illustration AO	-	Unknown
Illustration AP	-	www.neildoigphotography .co.uk

Chats with:

Mary Frail	-	Mary Frail
Nona Robb	-	Nona Robb
Bill Swan	-	from "Portrait of the East Neuk" by Peter Adamson
Ian Turnbull	-	Ian Turnbull
Ann Common	-	Ann Common
Andy Sherriff	-	Andy Sherriff, Anstruther

The illustrations that form the Picture Supplement (at the rear of the book) were kindly donated by the following suppliers:

The Windmill	-	www.Scran.ac.uk
The fire at Smith's dairy	-	University of St Andrews Library, Ref: GMC-19-33-4
The Milkmaids at Smith's farm	-	University of St Andrews Library, Ref: GMC-19-33-1

Other illustrations were supplied by:

Fife Council Archive centre
Jean Bell, Kingsbarns
Andy Sherriff, Anstruther
George Sutherland, St Andrews
Margaret Barrons, Kingsbarns
Messrs Pettigrew / Waterston (nee Anderson), Glasgow
Peter Atkin, Kingsbarns

Note: We have received many photographs and illustrations from a variety of people, publications, websites and other sources within the public domain. Whilst we have made every effort to acknowledge any copyright requirements where possible, we should apologise if we have inadvertently omitted to mention any originators of such photographs or illustrations.

North Street (now Smiddy Burn) in the 1920s.

The Barracks (centre of picture) off Seagate.

Kingsbarns windmill (thought to be at the North end of the village).

The Cambo Arms (now The Barns) – note the petrol pump in what is now the car park.

The village church – note the telegraph pole and lines which no longer exist, and the old bus which dates it around the 1930s.

The village church, in the form of a post card, from the early part of the 20th century.

Smith's dairy farm (now the B&B) after a fire in 1938

The Granary

Lady Wynd

Main Street (early 1900s) – note the shop/post office in the centre of the picture and the Stackyard (haystacks) in the right of the picture.

North Street (now Smiddy Burn) looking East in the early 1900s – note the paraffin street lamp on the right.

North Street (now Smiddy Burn) looking West in the early 1900s.

The old Village Hall.

Retreat Cottage in Bells Wynd.

Retreat Cottage in Bells Wynd

Seagate in the late 1800s/early 1900s.

Seagate looking East

The West end of Seagate.

The Stackyard in the early part of the 20th century.

The Stackyard now.

Station Road looking East.

Main Street in the 1930s – note the Auld Hoose in the foreground, the shop/post office in the background and the ability to walk along the "car-less" street.

Working on Wellgate in the Square

Working on Wellgate in The Square

The Pump in The Square

An artist's sketch of The Pump.

Flooding of Main Street, The Square and Station Road during underground excavation work in the mid 1900s.

Flooding of Main Street, The Square and Station Road during underground excavation work in the mid 1900s.

A footpath in the village – off Lady Wynd.

Anderson Place – off Lady Wynd.

The old Golf clubhouse in the 1930s.

The new Golf clubhouse now.

Kingsbarns harbour around 1910.

Kingsbarns harbour in the early 1900s.

The "swan-necks" of the wreck of HMS Success at low tide.

The mechanical parts of the wreck of HMS Success at low tide

Left to Right: Andrew Scott, George Martin, Tom Bell, Lawrence Brown, David Black. - Seagate 1932.

Milkmaids at Smiths farm (now the B&B and Kildinny Yards) in the 1930s.

Andy Sherriff the pretend farmer.

George Martin with his "tatties".

The farm horses ready for ploughing.

David Mayes (of Kippo) and his "decorated" horse at a village Flower Show during the 1930s.

Pipers at the village fete in 1932.

Robert Anderson, on holiday, at the village fair's coconut shy in 1932.

Dignitaries at the opening of a bygone village show

The Anderson and Gilmour children at the 1st tee of Kingsbarns golf course in the 1932 Children's Tournament.

The following 7 illustrations are period photographs of Kingsbarns School Pupils

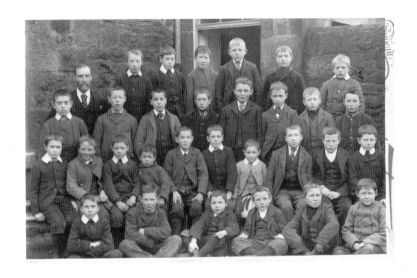

122

Kingsbarns Primary school pupils in 1957/8 (including members involved with this project: George Sutherland – front row 2nd from right and Andy Sherriff – back row 5th in from left).

Kildinny Yards in the snow of 2004.

North Quarter Steadings (previously the old Village Hall), The Barns and the Church in the snow of 2004.